THE
MESSIAH
in Early Judaism and Christianity

THE
MESSIAH
in Early Judaism and Christianity

Magnus Zetterholm, editor

Fortress Press
Minneapolis

THE MESSIAH
In Early Judaism and Christianity

Cover image: Three arches of the Golden Gate in Jerusalem. They are walled up and are supposed to open only upon the arrival of the Messiah. Photo © Erich Lessing / Art Resource, NY
Cover design: Josh Messner
Book design and typesetting: H. K. Scriptorium

Library of Congress Cataloging-in-Publication Data

The Messiah : in early Judaism and Christianity / Magnus Zetterholm, editor.
    p. cm.
  Includes bibliographical references and index.
  ISBN 978-0-8006-2108-7 (alk. paper)
  1. Messiah. 2. Messiah—Judaism. I. Zetterholm, Magnus, 1958-
BL475.M48 2007
296.3'36--dc22
                                2007008178

The paper used in this publication meets the minimum requirements of American National Standard for Information Sciences—Permanence of Paper for Printed Library Materials, ANSI Z329.48-1984.

Manufactured in the U.S.A.

10 09 08 07 06 1 2 3 4 5 6 7 8 9 10

CONTENTS

CONTRIBUTORS

Adela Yarbro Collins is the Buckingham Professor of New Testament Criticism and Interpretation at Yale Divinity School, New Haven, Conn. Her commentary on Mark in the Hermeneia series is scheduled for publication in the Fall of 2007. She is also the author of *Cosmology and Eschatology in Jewish and Christian Apocalypticism* (Brill, 1996), *The Beginning of the Gospel: Probings of Mark in Context* (Fortress, 1992), *Crisis and Catharsis: The Power of the Apocalypse* (Westminster, 1984), and *The Combat Myth in the Book of Revelation* (Scholars Press, 1976). She currently serves on the editorial boards of the *Journal for the Study of the New Testament*, *Biblical Interpretation*, and the *Catholic Biblical Quarterly*.

John J. Collins is the Holmes Professor of Old Testament Criticism and Interpretation at Yale Divinity School, New Haven, Conn. His more recent books include *Introduction to the Hebrew Bible* (Fortress, 2004), *Does the Bible Justify Violence?* (Fortress, 2004), *Jewish Cult and Hellenistic Culture* (Brill, 2005), *The Bible after Babel: Historical Criticism in a Postmodern Age* (Eerdmans, 2005), and *A Short Introduction to the Hebrew Bible* (Fortress, 2007). He has served as editor of the *Journal of Biblical Literature*, *Dead Sea Discoveries*, and the

Supplement Series to the *Journal for the Study of Judaism*; as president of the Catholic Biblical Association (1997) and as president of the Society of Biblical Literature (2002). He is coeditor of *The Encyclopedia of Apocalypticism* (Continuum).

Karin Hedner-Zetterholm is a Research Fellow in Jewish Studies, Centre for Theology and Religious Studies at Lund University, Lund, Sweden. She is the author of *Portrait of a Villain: Laban the Aramean in Rabbinic Literature* (Peeters, 2002) and several articles on rabbinic Judaism. She is currently working on a monograph on the role of Elijah in the rabbinic struggle for religious authority.

Jan-Eric Steppa is a Researcher in Church History and a board member of Collegium Patristicum Lundense at Lund University, Lund, Sweden. He is the author of the book *John Rufus and the World Vision of Anti-Chalcedonian Culture* (Gorgias Press, 2002), which explores the motives behind the opposition against the council of Chalcedon in 451.

Magnus Zetterholm is the Adjunct Associate Professor of New Testament Studies at Linköping University, Linköping, Sweden. He is the author of *The Formation of Christianity in Antioch: A Social-Scientific Approach to the Separation between Judaism and Christianity* (Routledge, 2003), and has also published numerous articles on the relations between Jews and non-Jews within the early Jesus movement, and a monograph (in Swedish) on the new views on Paul's relation to Judaism.

Acknowledgements

In May 2006, I had the pleasure of inviting Adela and John Collins, Yale Divinity School, to the Centre for Theology and Religious Studies at Lund University where I held a position as Research Fellow in New Testament Studies. In addition to the Collins' faculty lectures on messianism, I thought it would be a good idea to arrange a set of lectures for a somewhat wider audience. I engaged two of my colleagues, Jan-Eric Steppa and Karin Hedner-Zetterholm. We presented an overview of aspects of the development of messianism from the period of ancient Israelite religion to the patristic period and also covered several socio-historical contexts—early Judaism, the early Jesus movement, rabbinic Judaism, and emerging Christianity. The lectures from this small conference, *Aspects of Messianism in Early Judaism and Christianity*, are published in this volume, and I would like to express my gratitude to all my colleagues who contributed to this volume.

I also would like to thank the Centre for Theology and Religious Studies at Lund University for hosting this conference, and especially Bengt Holmberg, who was very supportive and enthusiastic about the idea of inviting Adela and John Collins and helped raise funds for financing the whole event. I also am indebted to Neil Elliott at Fortress for his patience and support.

Finally, I would like to dedicate my part of this work to Krister Stendahl, who made me realize that there was more to discover in Paul's letters than I had ever believed.

Magnus Zetterholm
February 2007

Abbreviations

Biblical Editions

LXX	Septuagint
NRSV	New Revised Standard Version

Old Testament Pseudepigrapha

2 Bar.	*2 Baruch (Syriac Apocalypse)*
1 En.	*1 Enoch (Ethiopic Apocalypse)*
Sib. Or.	*Sibylline Oracles*
T. Jud.	*Testament of Judah*
T. Levi	*Testament of Levi*

Apocrypha and Septuagint

Sir	Sirach/Ecclesiasticus
Tob	Tobit

Dead Sea Scrolls

CD	Cairo Genizah copy of the *Damascus Document*
1QIsa[a]	Isaiah[a]
1QM	*Milḥama (War Scroll)*
1QS	*Serek Hayaḥad (Rule of the Community)*
1QSa	*Rule of the Congregation* (Appendix a to 1QS)

1QSb	*Rule of the Blessings* (Appendix b to 1QS)
4Q174	*Florilegium*
4Q175	*Testimonia*
4Q246	*Apocryphon of Daniel*
4Q252	*Commentary on Genesis A*
4Q285	*Sefer Hamilḥamah*
4Q521	*Messianic Apocalypse*
11QMelch	*Melchizedek*

Mishnah, Talmud, and Related Literature

b.	Babylonian
m.	Mishnah
t.	Tosefta
y.	Jerusalem
B. Bat.	*Baba Batra*
B. Meṣiʿa	*Baba Meṣiʿa*
Ber.	*Berakot*
ʿErub.	*ʿErubin*
ʿEd.	*ʿEduyyot*
Giṭ.	*Giṭṭin*
Ḥag.	*Ḥagigah*
Hor.	*Horayot*
Ketub.	*Ketubbot*
Kil.	*Kilʾayim*
Pesaḥ.	*Pesaḥim*
Roš Haš.	*Roš Haššanah*
Šabb.	*Šabbat*
Sanh.	*Sanhedrin*
Šeqal.	*Šeqalim*
Taʿan.	*Taʿanit*

Other Rabbinic Works and Targumic Texts

Gen. Rab.	*Genesis Rabbah*
Lev. Rab.	*Leviticus Rabbah*
Pesiq. Rab.	*Pesiqta Rabbati*
Pirqe R. El.	*Pirqe Rabbi Eliezer*
S. ʿOlam Rab.	*Seder ʿOlam Rabbah*
Tg. Ps.-J.	*Targum Pseudo-Jonathan*

Classical Works

Athenagoras

| *Leg.* | *Legatio pro Christianis* |

Augustine
   Civ.   *De civitate Dei*

Epiphanius
   Pan.   *Panarion*

Eusebius
   Hist. eccl.   *Historia ecclesiastica*

Irenaeus
   Haer.   *Adversus haereses*

Jerome
   Comm. Isa.   *Commentariorum in Isaiam*

Josephus
   A.J.   *Antiquitates judaicae*
   B.J.   *Bellum judaicum*
   C. Ap.   *Contra Apionem*

Justin
   1 Apol.   *Apologia i*
   Dial.   *Dialogus cum Tryphone*

Minucius Felix
   Oct.   *Octavius*

Origen
   Cels.   *Contra Celsum*
   Hom. Judic. *Homiliae in Judices*
   Princ.   *De principiis*

Philo
   Praem.   *De praemeiis et poenis*
   Spec.   *De specialibus legibus*

Plato
   Phaed.   *Phaedo*

Pliny the Younger
   Ep.   *Epistulae*

Plutarch
   Num.   *Numa*

Suetonius
    Dom.   *Domitianus*

Tacitus
    Ann.   *Annales*

Tertullian
    Apol.   *Apologeticus*
    Marc.   *Adversus Marcionem*

Theophilus
    Autol.   *Ad Autolycum*

Secondary Sources

AB	Anchor Bible
ABRL	Anchor Bible Reference Library
ANF	*Ante-Nicene Fathers*
AOAT	Alter Orient und Altes Testament
BAG	Bauer, W., W. F. Arndt, and F. W. Gingrich. *Greek-English Lexicon of the New Testament and Other Early Christian Literature.* Chicago, 1957
BBR	*Bulletin for Biblical Research*
BETL	Bibliotheca ephemeridum theologicarum lovaniensium
BI	*Biblical Illustrator*
Bib	*Biblica*
BJS	Brown Judaic Studies
BNTC	Black's New Testament Commentaries
CBQ	*Catholic Biblical Quarterly*
CBQMS	Catholic Biblical Quarterly Monograph Series
CC	Continental Commentaries
ConBNT	Coniectanea biblica: New Testament Series
ConBOT	Coniectanea biblica: Old Testament Series
CRINT	Compendia rerum iudaicarum Novum Testamentum
DJD	Discoveries in the Judaean Desert
ExpTim	*Expository Times*
FOTL	Forms of the Old Testament Literature
HSM	Harvard Semitic Monographs
HTR	*Harvard Theological Review*
HUCM	Monographs of the Hebrew Union College
ICC	International Critical Commentary
JBL	*Journal of Biblical Literature*
JECS	*Journal of Early Christian Studies*

JSJ	*Journal for the Study of Judaism in the Persian, Hellenistic, and Roman Periods*
JSNT	*Journal for the Study of the New Testament*
JSNTSup	Journal for the Study of the New Testament: Supplement Series
JSOT	*Journal for the Study of the Old Testament*
JSOTSup	Journal for the Study of the Old Testament: Supplement Series
JSPSup	Journal for the Study of the Pseudepigrapha: Supplement Series
JSQ	*Jewish Studies Quarterly*
JTS	*Journal of Theological Studies*
LCL	Loeb Classical Library
Neot	*Neotestamentica*
NPNF²	*Nicene and Post-Nicene Fathers*, Series 2
NTS	*New Testament Studies*
OBO	Orbis biblicus et orientalis
Or	*Orientalia* (NS)
OTP	*Old Testament Pseudepigrapha*. Edited by J. H. Charlesworth. 2 vols. New York, 1983, 1985
RB	*Revue biblique*
SBLDS	Society of Biblical Literature Dissertation Series
SBLEJL	Society of Biblical Literature Early Judaism and Its Literature
SBLMS	Society of Biblical Literature Monograph Series
SBT	Studies in Biblical Theology
SEÅ	*Svensk exegetisk årsbok*
STDJ	*Studies on the Texts of the Deserts of Judah*
StPatr	Studia patristica
TSAJ	Texte und Studien zum antiken Judentum
VC	*Vigiliae christianae*
WUNT	Wissenschaftliche Untersuchungen zum Neuen Testament

TIMELINE

2000–1700 BCE	widely accepted by scholars as the time span for the patriarchal figures of Genesis
1700–1300 BCE	widely accepted by scholars as the time span for the sojourn of Hebrew groups in Egypt
1300–1200 BCE	migration of Hebrew groups from Egypt (the "Exodus") some time during this century
1200–1050 BCE	the formation of the people of Israel in Canaan
ca 1000–ca 960 BCE	reign of David
922 BCE	Israel divided into Northern and Southern Kingdoms
722 BCE	fall of the Northern Kingdom (Israel) to Assyria
587 BCE	fall of the Southern Kingdom (Judah) to Babylon: beginning of the Babylonian exile
539 BCE	some exiles return to Judah from Babylonia under Persian control; beginning of the Persian period
333 BCE	Alexander the Great defeats the Persians at Issus; beginning of the Hellenistic period; in 332 Alexander captures Jerusalem
167–63 BCE	The Maccabean period: in 167 the priest Mattathias and his five sons begin the so-called Maccabean revolt against the Seleucid Empire; in 164 the Maccabees rededicate the temple in Jerusalem (*Hanukkah*)
142–63 BCE	Jewish self-rule in Palestine under the Hasmoneans, descendants of Mattathias
63 BCE	The Roman general Pompey captures Jerusalem
37–4 BCE	reign of Herod the Great, a client king of Rome, in Judea

31 BCE	Octavian (later Augustus) defeats Marc Anthony in the battle of Actium, widely regarded as the end of the Hellenistic period and the beginning of the Roman period (note that *culturally* the Hellenistic legacy continues through the 6th century CE)
27 BCE–14 CE	reign of the Roman emperor Augustus
ca 5 BCE	birth of Jesus of Nazareth
14–37	reign of the Roman emperor Tiberius
ca 33	Jesus of Nazareth executed by Romans
37–41	reign of the Roman emperor Caligula
41–54	reign of the Roman emperor Claudius
ca 50–55	Paul writes his letters
54–68	reign of the Roman emperor Nero
66–70	first Jewish war against the Romans
70	Romans capture Jerusalem, destroying the city and the Temple
ca 70–ca 100	period during which the four canonical Gospels are written
132–135	the Bar Kokhba revolt, the second Jewish war against the Romans
ca 200	final redaction of the Mishnah by Yehudah Ha-Nasi
311	the Roman emperor Galerius issues an edict of toleration for all religions, including Christianity
313	the Roman emperor Constantine the Great issues an edict at Milan, stating that the Empire should be neutral with regard to all religions
325	the Council of Nicea, convoked to settle the issue of Jesus' divinity, declares Jesus the Son equal to, one with, and of the same substance as God the Father
380	Christianity becomes the religion of the Roman empire
381	the First Council of Constantinople confirms the decisions of the council of Nicea and defines the divinity of the Holy Spirit
ca 400	final redaction of the Jerusalem Talmud
431	the Council of Ephesus declares the Virgin Mary as Theotokos, "Mother of God"
451	the Council of Chalcedon deals with the relation between Jesus' human and divine natures, defining Jesus as one person (*hypostasis*) in two natures (*ousiai*), human and divine
5th–7th century	final redaction of the Babylonian Talmud

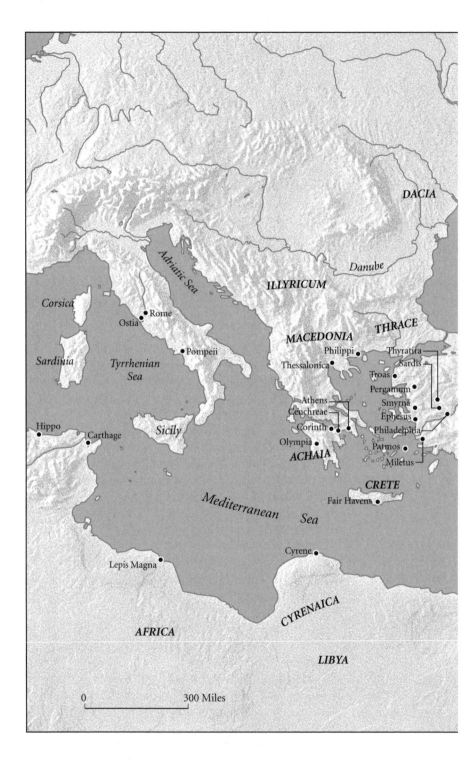

DACIA

Adriatic Sea

Danube

ILLYRICUM

Corsica

Rome
Ostia

MACEDONIA

THRACE

Philippi

Phyratira

Sardis

Sardinia

*Tyrrhenian
Sea*

Pompeii

Thessalonica

Troas

Pergamum

Smyrna

Athens

Ephesus

Hippo

Cenchreae

Philadelphia

Carthage

Sicily

Corinth

Patmos

Olympia

ACHAIA

Miletus

CRETE

Mediterranean   Sea

Fair Havens

Cyrene

Lepis Magna

CYRENAICA

AFRICA

LIBYA

0   300 Miles

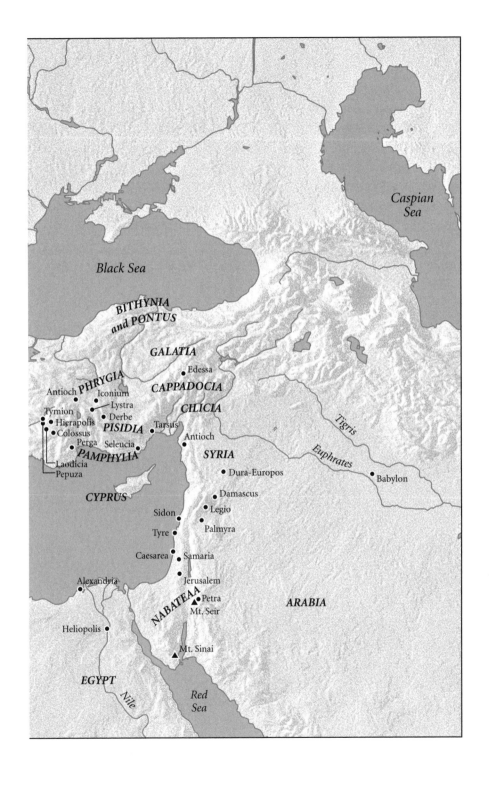

Caspian
Sea

Black Sea

BITHYNIA
and PONTUS

GALATIA

Edessa

PHRYGIA

CAPPADOCIA

Antioch   Iconium

Tymion   Lystra   CILICIA

Hierapolis   Derbe

Colossus   PISIDIA   Tarsus

Perga   Seleucia   Antioch

Laodicia   PAMPHYLIA   SYRIA

Pepuza

CYPRUS   Dura-Europos

Damascus

Sidon   Legio

Tyre   Palmyra

Caesarea   Samaria

Alexandria

Jerusalem

Petra   ARABIA

NABATEAA   Mt. Seir

Heliopolis

Mt. Sinai

EGYPT   Nile

Red
Sea

Tigris

Euphrates

Babylon

INTRODUCTION

Magnus Zetterholm

In the history of religions, the idea of a messianic figure must be regarded as a very successful notion and, indeed, a very flexible one. Its origin can be traced back to a common Near Eastern royal ideology, where the king was considered to have a very special status in relation to the gods and sometimes was thought to have a divine origin. In ancient Israel, however, the concept of the Messiah, "the anointed one," was connected to King David in particular. In spite of his human fallibility, King David became the primary role model to which messianic expectations were connected, and the throne of David was thought to last forever.

It is likely that the trauma caused by the fall of Jerusalem in 587/586 BCE, and the subsequent deportation of the population, gave rise to messianic expectations during the post-exilic period. The fact that Jerusalem was destroyed and that there was no Israelite king on the throne called for a hermeneutical reinterpretation of the whole idea of a Davidic kingdom. The first stage in this process was the hope for a reestablishment of the Davidic throne, a

development clearly detectable in parts of the prophetic tradition. The Hasmonean assumption of power during the
second century BCE made people realize that an autonomous
kingdom was possible but that the Hasmonean concentra-
tion of power was far from being the ideal Davidic kingdom.
This situation led to a revitalization of messianic expectations but also caused the messianic idea to develop along
new lines.

While the dream of an earthly kingdom continued to live
on, the notion of God's Messiah simultaneously was
affected by eschatological and apocalyptic trends within
Second Temple Judaism. The original idea of a Davidic
kingdom was transformed into something very different—
the expectation of a superhuman, angelic savior connected
to ideas of the dawn of a new age and the establishment of
the eschatological kingdom of God.

In the beginning of the first century CE, the idea of God's
Messiah took another and unexpected turn, also motivated
by a significant crisis, but of a rather different kind. Within
a small Jewish group in the Land of Israel, messianic expectations were connected to a young Jewish teacher—Jesus of
Nazareth. His execution by the Romans in the early 30s led
to a severe crisis of meaning among his followers. Even
though there was a rich supply of culturally determined
messianic traditions, none of these included the suffering
and death of the Messiah of Israel. To identity Jesus of
Nazareth with the Messiah, the early Jesus movement had
to redefine the role and function of the Messiah. Through
an advanced application of Jewish hermeneutics, the Jesus
movement was able to bring new meanings to the biblical
texts, and the Davidic Messiah of Israel was transformed
into the risen Savior, the Lord of heaven and earth.

One peculiar feature of the Jesus movement was the idea
that Jesus' death and resurrection also provided means for
the salvation of the Gentile nations. Thus, parts of the
movement began an extensive mission initially among

those non-Jews who participated in the activities of the Jewish communities in the Diaspora. However, in the beginning of the second century and due to a combination of historical and political-religious circumstances, the non-Jewish part of the Jesus movement began to define itself in opposition to Judaism. Christianity, as a non- and even anti-Jewish religion, emerged, and for the first time, the concept of the Messiah began to develop in a non-Jewish ideological context.

In this predominantly Greco-Roman milieu, the concept of the Messiah underwent its third major transformation. This development, however, took place from new points of departure. Partly disconnected from its Jewish roots, the idea of the Messiah was interpreted by means of Greek philosophy, and the specifically Christian concept of the Messiah was challenged and criticized by individuals representing pagan religion, philosophy, and society. Furthermore, the political development in the Roman Empire led the church to start asking new questions regarding the Messiah. Thus, one of the most important questions during the first centuries was related to Jesus' divinity and his relation to God. After harsh and poignant conflicts, mainstream Christianity finally reached an agreement regarding the nature of Christ, as stated in the doctrine of the Trinity and the Creed of Nicea. During the fourth century, Jesus Christ, the Messiah, the Son of God, the anointed one, became God himself. The Messiah of Israel found a completely new and unexpected setting—as the Messiah of the church and of the Roman Empire.

At the same time, messianism continued to develop within a Jewish framework. During the Tannaitic period, messianism seems to have flourished primarily in popular folk tradition while being suppressed by the religious elite. During the Amoraic period, however, the rabbis integrated messianic elements with their own religious tradition. The Messiah of Israel was transformed again, this time into a tool for promoting the rabbis' Torah-centered worldview. The arrival of the Messiah was made dependent on observance of the Torah as interpreted by the rabbis, and any political features of messianism were effectively downplayed for quite obvious reasons.

In contemporary Judaism, messianism generally plays a minor role. The view traditionally held by many Christians that there is a fundamental opposition between the Torah and faith in Jesus Christ, between Judaism and Christianity, and the historical consequences of this ideology may, at least in part, explain this standpoint. Nonetheless, within some parts of modern Judaism, the Messiah still remains an important figure. The best-known example is perhaps the ultra-Orthodox movement Chabad, which caused some turmoil within the Jewish community by attributing various degrees of messianic status to their rebbe, Menachem Mendel Schneersohn. In Israel a tiny minority with ideological connections to Gush Emunim, the settler movement, also is influenced by messianic expectations. In its view, settling every inch of the Land of Israel is an important means to bring the Messiah.

Thus, a concept of a Messiah exists both within Judaism, where it originated, and in Christianity, where perhaps it underwent its most profound transformation. But contrary to what is often assumed, messianism scarcely constitutes a common ground for Jews and Christians and is certainly not the best starting point for Jewish-Christian relations. Rather, due to the unfortunate historical development of Jewish-Christian relations, "the Messiah" has been the most important concept that *distinguishes* Christianity from Judaism. The indisputable historical fact that the Jewish people, in general, do not accept Jesus as the Messiah of Israel traditionally has been a major reason for Christians condemning Jews. One of the earliest examples of this is the homily *Peri Pascha* (late second century) of Melito of Sardis. Melito not only accuses the Jews of repudiating Jesus, but also of being responsible for killing him, which Melito considers equal to murdering God.

Against this background, it is hardly surprising that some Jewish critics of Chabad's messianism have gone as far as questioning whether or not Chabad could still be considered a form of Judaism. Still, it is hard not to be astounded (and distressed) over the following development: a Jewish interpretation of the Messiah eventually gave rise to a non-Jewish religion, Christianity, which used the concept to renounce its roots, resulting in a situation where contemporary Jewish messianic ideas lead to marginalization vis-à-vis mainstream Judaism.

The many historical manifestations of messianic figures, and the complicated and long development in several theological and sociohistorical contexts, suggest something about the complexity of the messianic phenomenon. There never has and never will be one distinct definition of "the Messiah." Furthermore, even though it is evident that Jewish and Christian messianic interpretations differ fundamentally on some vital points, it is clear that both traditions have moved a long way from their respective origins. This is, of course, quite natural. Theological concepts are never static but are incessantly involved in an ongoing dialectical transformation process determined by the needs of the religious community and the development in a constantly changing world. Regarding the concept of the Messiah, this is quite evident.

Awareness of this may, of course, help us understand the past but could also give us hope for the future. The suppleness of the idea of the Messiah and its tendency to adapt to new circumstances may suggest that the prevalent incompatibility of Jewish and Christian interpretations of messianism also could change. The extensive reorientation that has taken place within New Testament scholarship since the latter part of the nineteenth century regarding the historical setting of Jesus of Nazareth has resulted in an increased emphasis on Jesus' Jewishness rather than his uniqueness. A corresponding paradigm shift may be on its way with regard to Paul's relation to Judaism. Today, an increasing number of scholars work from the assumption that Paul never broke away from Judaism but opposed non-Jewish involvement in the Torah. The former tendency within New Testament scholarship to define Christianity in opposition to Judaism has been replaced by a search for affinity and the common origin of both religions.

These new trends within New Testament scholarship imply that the concept of the Messiah could soon be involved in a new process of theological revision and development. Such a process would, for instance, be essential for further development of Jewish-Christian relations. There can be no doubt that some aspects of the Christian interpretation of the Messiah have functioned as an effective tool for promoting an ideology that resulted in persecution and marginalization of the Jewish people. In the future, it is possible that some aspects of messianism will become common ground for Jewish and Christian theological reflection. But whatever the outcome of such a potential process, it seems clear that an adaptation to these new circumstances would be quite in line with the dynamic nature of messianism.

The present volume provides a comprehensive diachronic introduction to the emergence and early development of some of the vital aspects of messianism in Judaism and Christianity in several sociohistorical contexts. The introductory survey of the origin and early development of Jewish messianism during the biblical and postbiblical periods (John J. Collins) becomes the starting point for two essays on the reinterpretation and development of the idea of the Messiah within the predominantly Jewish Jesus movement (Adela Yarbro Collins, Magnus Zetterholm). Following these is an essay on the understanding of messianism within rabbinic Judaism after the extensive changes brought about by the crisis following the fall of Jerusalem

(Karin Hedner-Zetterholm). In the concluding essay, another important context is brought into focus: the reception and transformation of messianic ideas with the rise of Christianity as a non-Jewish religion (Jan-Eric Steppa). These are the main contexts in which the changing faces of the Jewish and Christian Messiah have developed—and, in fact, are still developing.

1

PRE-CHRISTIAN JEWISH MESSIANISM: AN OVERVIEW

John J. Collins

The word "messiah" in modern parlance is roughly synonymous with "savior." In scholarly usage, it is somewhat
more specific than that. The Hebrew word from which it is
derived, *māšîaḥ*, means "anointed one." It is used in the
Hebrew Bible both for kings and high priests,[1] who were in
fact anointed, and in the Dead Sea Scrolls, it also is used
metaphorically with reference to prophets.[2] It does not have
a future or eschatological connotation in the Hebrew Bible.[3]
In the Second Temple period when there was no longer a
king on the throne, the term as applied to a king came to
refer to the one who would restore the kingship and usher
in the eschatological age. The same figure also could be des-
ignated by other terms, such as "branch of David."[4] Ideal,
even supernatural, characteristics were often attributed to
him. As we shall see, the word *māšîaḥ*, even in an eschatological context, was used to refer to a priest as well as to a

king. Nonetheless, the default reference of the term is to the legitimate, Davidic king of Israel at the end of days.

Royal Ideology

The messianic ideal has its roots in ancient Near Eastern royal ideology. The importance of the monarchy is dramatized in the Babylonian creation myth, *Enuma Elish*. The champion god Marduk confronts the threat posed by the monster goddess Tiamat, and in return he is named "king of the gods."[5] In the Ugaritic myths, monarchy is dramatized by the story of Ba'al.[6] In Egypt, the Pharaoh was thought to be son of the sun-god, Re, and some texts from the New Kingdom period describe his begetting in sexual terms.[7] In Mesopotamia and Canaan, the king also was said to be the son of a god, but there was less emphasis on his divinity.[8]

Traces of similar royal ideology survive in the Psalms. According to Ps 2, the Lord set his king (also called his anointed) on Zion and commanded him to rule in the midst of his enemies. He also tells him: "You are my son; today I have begotten you" (v. 7). When the nations plot against the king, the Lord laughs and scorns them. A reference to divine begetting also should be restored in Ps 110:3. The Hebrew is corrupt, but it should be restored, following the Greek, to read: "I have begotten you" (perhaps: "from the womb, from dawn, you have the dew with which I have begotten you").[9] The Lord invites the king to sit at his right hand and make his enemies his footstool and also tells him that he is a priest forever according to the order of Melchizedek (king of Salem/Jerusalem in the time of Abraham). Both the motif of recognition ("you are my son") and the enthronement on the right hand are Egyptian motifs,[10] although Melchizedek was a Canaanite king. Jerusalem was subject to Egypt in pre-Israelite times, and it is likely that old formulae and traditions were taken over by the kings of Judah.[11] The king is addressed as *ʾĕlōhîm*, "god," in Ps 45:6, although he is clearly subordinate to the Most High ("your god," v. 7). Other Psalms ascribe extraordinary divine blessing to the king. So Ps 21:4: "He asked you for life; you gave it to him—length of days forever and ever." Whether this should be taken to imply that at least some kings were granted immortality or should be taken as hyperbolic, is not clear.[12]

The Promise to David

The special status of the king was confirmed in the promise to David in 2 Sam 7. This passage is embedded in the Deuteronomistic history,[13] and so the formulation is relatively late, perhaps exilic, but it preserves an old tradition.[14] On the one hand, it declares the king to be a son of God (7:14a: "I will be a father to him and he will be a son to me") and promises that the kingship will never be taken away from the house of David (7:16: "your house and your kingdom shall be made sure forever before me; your throne shall be established forever"). On the other hand, it acknowledges the humanity of the king: "when he commits iniquity, I will punish him with a rod such as mortals use" (7:14b). This threat of punishment is a far cry from the rhetoric of the Egyptian kings. The main importance of the promise was that it seemed to guarantee that there would always be a descendant of David on the throne in Jerusalem. After the capture of Jerusalem by the Babylonians in 586 BCE, however, this was no longer the case. The cognitive dissonance caused by the discrepancy between the divine promise and the present reality is the root of messianic expectation.

Messianic Expectation in the Prophets?[15]

The prophet who concerned himself most with the Jerusalem kingship was Isaiah.[16] Isaiah 7:14 ("the young woman is with child and will bear a son") was a sign of hope to King Ahaz about the future of the royal line. The child in question often is identified as Hezekiah (also in rabbinic tradition),[17] but he is not necessarily a future king. In any case, he is not a messiah and was not interpreted as one in Jewish tradition. The poem in Isa 9 ("for a child has been born for us, a son given to us") is most probably a poem for the enthronement of a king, perhaps Hezekiah.[18] The titles given to this "child" — "Wonderful Counselor, Mighty God, Everlasting Father, Prince of Peace" — conform to the royal ideology in ascribing divinity, in some sense, to the king.[19] Here again the king in question belongs to the present rather than the future. In Isa 11:1–9, however, there is a genuine messianic oracle that predicts "a shoot from the stump of Jesse" who will usher in a wonderful age when the wolf will live with the lamb. There is no consensus as to when this oracle was composed. The reference to the "stump of Jesse" implies that the "tree" was cut down. Nonetheless some scholars think that the oracle may come from Isaiah.[20] Others see this as a reference to the assassination of King Amon, father of Josiah (2 Kgs 21:23), and see the wonderful king as Josiah, who was only eight years old when he began to reign (cf. Isa 11:6: "a little child shall lead them").[21] Many scholars, however, think that the "stump" presupposes the definitive fall of the Davidic kingship to the Babylonians in 586 BCE and see the "shoot" as a figure wished for in the utopian future.[22]

Similar ambiguity attends to the prophecy in Amos 9:11 about the fallen booth of David. Here again some scholars have defended its authenticity as an eighth-century prophecy.[23] Others regard it as transparently postexilic.[24]

Equally uncertain is the provenance of the oracle in Mic 5:2 that refers to a future ruler of Israel to come from Bethlehem.[25] This oracle implies a critique of the Jerusalem kingship, but not a rejection of the Davidic line. Rather, it calls for a new beginning, in humble circumstances. Such a critique could have been made while there was a king in Jerusalem, but it also could have originated during or after the exile, with the implication that it was the arrogance of the rulers in Jerusalem that led to the fall.

Jeremiah, who prophesied at the time of the Babylonian invasion, was famously critical of the rulers of his day. His oracle on the occasion of the deportation of King Jehoiachin in 597 BCE seems to ring the death knell for the Davidic dynasty: "Record this man as childless . . . for none of his offspring shall succeed in sitting on the throne of David and ruling again in Judah" (Jer 22:30). A king, however, could be a descendant of David without being a descendant of Jehoiachin. (He was in fact succeeded by his uncle Zedekiah.) According to the following chapter in Jeremiah, "the days are coming, says the Lord, when I shall raise up for David a righteous branch, and he shall reign as king and deal wisely, and shall execute justice and righteousness in the land . . . and this is the name by which he will be called, 'the Lord is our righteousness'" (Jer 23:6). The latter expression (*YHWH ṣidqēnû*) appears to be a play on the name of Zedekiah.[26] Whether the oracle should be read as affirming Zedekiah as a righteous king or rather as saying that only a future king will live up to Zedekiah's name is uncertain, but the latter seems more likely in view of the general tenor of Jeremiah's prophecy. This oracle is further updated in Jer 33:14–16, which says that the branch will be raised up "in those days and at that time."[27] This passage is not found in the Greek translation of Jeremiah and is almost certainly an addition to the Hebrew text from some time in the post-exilic period.

The future restoration of the Davidic line is also affirmed in Ezekiel, where the future king is usually, but not exclusively, referred to as *nāśîʾ* ("prince") rather than as king.[28] In Ezekiel's vision of the new Jerusalem, however, the role of the king is greatly reduced. He is primarily responsible for providing the offerings for the temple service.[29]

One other prophetic passage that predicts a future restoration of the kingship should be noted. Zechariah 9:9 tells Jerusalem, "Lo your king comes to you; triumphant and victorious is he, humble and riding on a donkey, on a colt, the foal of a donkey." The donkey was the preferred means of transport of tribal leaders in the period of the Judges. The reference here is a throwback to that time and implies the rejection of the horse, the favored animal in warfare. The Masoretic text refers to "sons of Greece" as the adversaries of the sons of Zion in 9:13 and for that reason, many scholars have dated this oracle to the time of Alexander the Great.[30] The reading is doubtful, however, and there is no consensus on the provenance of this passage.[31] It is noteworthy that some messianic oracles (also Mic 5) express disillusionment with the attempts of kings to engage in warfare and look instead for someone who will rely on divine help.

When Jews were allowed to return from Babylon and rebuild the temple, there seems to have been a brief flurry of messianic expectation associated with the figure of Zerubbabel (Hag 1–2; Zech 1–6).[32] Haggai tells Zerubbabel that the Lord is about to overthrow nations and make him like a signet ring. Zechariah says that the Lord is going to bring "my servant the branch" (Zech 3:8), an apparent reference to Jeremiah's prophecy. It is possible that the oracle in Jeremiah is a late addition and presupposes Zechariah. Zerubbabel's name means "shoot of Babylon." Zechariah 6:12 announces the arrival of the branch: "here is a man whose name is Branch." These words were almost certainly addressed to Zerubbabel, but his name has been excised from the text, so that the words now seem to be addressed to the high priest Joshua. Zerubbabel disappears abruptly from history. The Persians allowed the Jews to rebuild their temple, but they were not prepared to accept a restored Jewish kingdom. Second Isaiah was perhaps more realistic than Haggai and Zechariah when he said that Cyrus of Persia, who was neither Davidic nor Jewish, was the *māšîaḥ* of the Lord (Isa 45:1).

The Septuagint

It is clear enough that some messianic prophecies were introduced into the biblical text in the postexilic period. These prophecies, however, are difficult to date, and so we have no clear picture of the extent of messianic expectation in the Persian or early Hellenistic period. One possible window into the early Hellenistic period is provided by the Greek translation of the Bible, the Septuagint, of which the Pentateuch was translated by the mid-third century BCE. Despite some claims to the contrary,[33] the LXX Pentateuch provides little evidence of messianic expectation.[34] The pentateuchal passage that was most often read as a messianic prediction in ancient Judaism is an enigmatic passage in the blessing of Jacob, Gen 49:10: "until Shiloh comes, and the obedience of the people is his." The majority reading of the LXX manuscripts translates *šîlōh* as "the things laid away for him" and fails to associate the future glory of Judah with an individual ruler. The Greek version of Balaam's oracles (Num 24:7, 17) speaks of a "man," who will have a kingdom, and this is of some significance for messianism in the Hellenistic period, even though this passage refrains from calling him a king. Of course, the Pentateuch did not provide many opportunities for the translators to indulge in messianic speculation. The situation is different in the Prophets and Psalms, which were translated later (second or first century BCE). Passages such as Isa 11 were translated faithfully, but there also were some cases where the translators introduced messianic references without foundation in the Hebrew text.[35] For example, in Amos 4:13, the Lord reveals to humanity "what is his thought" (*mah-śēḥō*). The Greek reads: "announcing to humanity his anointed" (*ton christon autou*). The translator may have misread the Hebrew letters, but he evidently found it plausible that the Lord should be spoken of as announcing his anointed. Moreover, texts such as Ps 2 that originally referred to a historical king were now presumably read as referring to a king who was to come, in effect, an eschatological messiah.[36]

The Dead Sea Scrolls

Since the promise to David was part of received Scripture, it is unlikely that it ever lapsed entirely, but the testimonies for much of the Second Temple period are very sparse. Several major works (Chronicles, Ezra-Nehemiah, Sirach) show no interest in messianic expectation. More remarkable is the lack of clear references to the messiah in the early apocalypses of Enoch and Daniel in the early second century BCE. The "one like a son of man" in Dan 7 receives a kingdom on behalf of the people, but he is most plausibly understood as an angelic figure rather than as a Davidic messiah (of whom there is no other indication in Daniel; the word *māšîaḥ* is used twice in Dan 9:25–26 with reference to priestly leaders, although these references were later reinterpreted as messianic). It would seem then that messianic interpretation was largely dormant from the early Hellenistic period to the time of the Maccabean revolt.

The Branch of David

In contrast, the Dead Sea Scrolls, which were written mainly in the first half of the first century BCE, provide ample though fragmentary evidence of a revival of messianic expectation under the Hasmoneans.[37] Much of this evidence is found in exegetical contexts.[38] The pesher on Isaiah cites Isa 11:1–5 and comments: "The interpretation of the matter concerns the branch of David, who will arise at the end of days." The context refers to a battle with the

Kittim, a name (derived from Citium in Cyprus) that may refer either to Greeks or Romans but refers to Romans in the *pesharim*. A fragment of the War Rule, 4Q285, also refers to "Isaiah the prophet" and cites Isa 11:1 ("there shall come forth a shoot from the stump of Jesse"). Another line reads "the branch of David, and they will enter into judgment with. . . ." The branch—the word used in Jeremiah is *ṣemaḥ*—is apparently taken as the fulfillment of Isaiah's prophecy about the shoot from the stump of Jesse. Another fragmentary line reads, "the Prince of the Congregation, the bran[ch of David] will kill him" (this verse was initially read as "they will kill the Prince of the Congregation, the bran[ch of David]," but in all the parallel passages, and in Isa 11 itself, the messianic figure does the killing). While the word *māšîaḥ* does not occur in either the pesher or 4Q285, there is little doubt that the branch of David is the messianic king.

In 4Q252 (pesher on Genesis), the branch is explicitly called *māšîaḥ* in the context of an interpretation of Gen 49:10:

> Whenever Israel rules there shall [not] fail to be a descendant of David upon the throne. For the ruler's staff is the covenant of kingship, [and the clans] of Israel are the feet, until the Messiah of Righteousness comes, the branch of David. For to him and to his seed was granted the covenant of kingship over his people for everlasting generations.

The phrase "Messiah of Righteousness" echoes the "righteous branch" of Jeremiah.

The fragment 4Q285 also shows that the "Prince of the Congregation" was none other than the branch of David. This also should be apparent from the *Rule of the Blessings* (1QSb), which includes a blessing for the Prince that draws heavily on Isa 11:

> The Master shall bless the Prince of the Congrega-
> tion . . . and shall renew for him the Covenant of the

Community that he may establish the kingdom of
His people for ever, [that he may judge the poor with
righteousness and] dispense justice with equity to
the oppressed of the land. (Isa 11:4b)

The blessing continues:

[May you smite the peoples] with the might of your
hand and ravage the earth with your scepter; may
you bring death to the ungodly with the breath of
your lips" (Isa 11:4b). ["May He shed upon you the
spirit of counsel] and everlasting might, the spirit of
knowledge and of the fear of God; may righteousness be the girdle [of your loins] and may your reins
be girded [with faithfulness]. (Isa 11:5)

It goes on to compare the prince to a young bull with horns
of iron and hooves of bronze and probably also to a lion (cf.
Gen 49:9). Also notable is the statement, "for God has established you as the scepter," which is probably an allusion to
Balaam's oracle in Num 24:17.

The branch of David also appears in the *Florilegium*
(4Q174). This fragmentary text strings together commentaries on 2 Sam 7:10–14; Ps 1:1, and Ps 2:1. Second Samuel
7:14 ("I will be a father to him and he will be a son to me")
is said to refer to "the branch of David, who shall arise with
the Interpreter of the Law in Zion at the end of days." Also,
we are told that "the fallen tent of David" (Amos 9:11) is
"he who shall arise to save Israel."

The Prince of the Congregation also appears with messianic overtones in CD 7:18 (the *Damascus Document* from
the Cairo Geniza) in the context of a citation of Balaam's
oracle from Num 24. The two manuscripts of CD have different texts at this point. In ms A, citations of Amos 5:26–27,
which mentions Kaiwan your star-god, and Amos 9:11 are
followed by Num 24:17:

The star is the Interpreter of the Law who shall come
to Damascus, as it is written, A star shall come forth
out of Jacob and a scepter shall rise out of Israel. The
scepter is the Prince of the whole Congregation, and
when he comes he shall smite all the children of
Sheth.

The messianic interpretation of Balaam's oracle is well
attested. The most famous example is the story where
Rabbi Akiba thought that the star was Simon bar Kosiba,
who led the revolt against Rome in 132 CE and was thereafter known as Bar Kochba, son of the star (*y. Ta'an.* 68d).
As we have seen, the LXX translates "scepter" as "man,"
and Philo of Alexandria says that this "man" is a warrior
who will subdue great nations" (*Praem.* 95). Philo's familiarity with this interpretation of Balaam's oracle is all the
more significant because he was not generally interested in
messianism. The star and scepter are also interpreted mes-
sianically in *T. Jud.* 24:1–6. In the *Damascus Document,* the
star and scepter are taken as two separate figures. Balaam's
oracle is cited without interpretation in the *Testimonia*
(4Q175) and in 1QM 11:6–7.

The picture of the Davidic messiah that emerges from the
passages we have discussed so far is one of a mighty warrior who would drive out the Gentiles. This picture is based
on a small network of biblical prophecies, most promi-
nently Isa 11, Gen 49, Jer 23 (the branch), and Balaam's oracle. This picture was in no way peculiar to the sect of the
Scrolls. The *Psalms of Solomon,* extant in Greek but probably
composed in Hebrew around the middle of the first century
BCE, are often thought to be Pharisaic in origin.[39] *Psalms of
Solomon* 17 recalls the promise to David and complains that
"those to whom you did not make the promise" have
"despoiled the throne of David." These people are not Gentiles but the Hasmonean rulers (descended from the Maccabees), who had declared themselves kings at the end of

the second century BCE. Their kingdom lasted about forty years, until the Roman general Pompey captured Jerusalem in 63 BCE. The *Psalms of Solomon* are bitterly critical of the Hasmoneans and pray that God will restore a descendant of David:

> Undergird him with the strength to destroy the
>   unrighteous rulers,
> to purge Jerusalem from gentiles
> who trample her to destruction;
> in wisdom and in righteousness [cf. Isa 11] to drive
>   out
> the sinners from the inheritance
> to smash the arrogance of sinners like a potter's jar
>   (Ps 2:9)
> to shatter all their substance with an iron rod (Ps 2:9)
> to destroy the unlawful nations with the word of his
>   mouth. (Isa 11:4)

This picture of a warrior messiah was shared across sectarian lines and was even reflected in the writings of Philo of Alexandria.

The *Psalms of Solomon* also provide a clue as to why there was a revival of messianic expectation in the early first century BCE. The Hasmoneans had renewed native Jewish kingship, but they were not descendants of David. Hence the desire by various opposition groups that the Lord would raise up a Davidic king, rather than one of those to whom the promise had not been given.

Two Messiahs

The messianic expectation of the Scrolls was distinctive, however, in another respect.[40] The *Rule of the Community* (*Serek Hayaḥad*, 1QS) says that the men of the community should depart from none of the rules "until there shall come a prophet and the messiahs of Aaron and Israel (*měšîḥēy ʾahărŏn wěyiśrāēl*) (1QS 9:11). The *Damascus Document* uses a similar expression: *māšîaḥ ʾahărŏn wĕyîśrāēl.* The latter expression sometimes has been read as a singular, but it is not apparent why one messiah should be said to be from both Aaron and Israel. Moreover, several other scrolls pair the messiah of Israel with another figure. *Rule of the Congregation* (1QSa), the eschatological rule for the end of days, insists that the messiah of Israel should not extend his hand to the bread before the priest says grace. In the pesher on Isaiah, the statement in Isa 11:3 that the messiah "shall not judge by what his eyes see" is taken to mean that he will defer to "priests of renown." In the *Florilegium*, the branch of David is accompanied by the Interpreter of the Law, and likewise in CD 7:19, the Prince of the Congregation is linked with the Interpreter. In the Temple Scroll, too, the king is clearly subject to the authority of the priests.

The idea of two messiahs has a biblical precedent in the "two sons of oil," interpreted as two anointed ones, most probably Zerubbabel and the high priest Joshua, in Zech 4:14. It reflects the priestly character of the sect of the Dead Sea Scrolls, which valued the priesthood even more highly than the messianic kingship. But this feature of messianic expectation in the Scrolls also may be explained by opposition to the Hasmoneans. Not only had the latter appropriated the kingship to which they had no traditional right, they also had appropriated the high priesthood and combined the offices of king and high priest. Even though Ps 110 told the king that he was a priest forever after the order of Melchizedek, the sectarians whose views are reflected in the Scrolls held firmly that the two offices should be distinct. Hence their hope for two messiahs at the end of days.

Controversial Texts

Three other texts from the Dead Sea Scrolls require comment: 4Q246, 4Q521, and 4Q541. 4Q246 is popularly known as "the Son of God" text. The text consists of two columns, of which the first is torn down the middle so that only the second half of the lines survives.[41] Someone is said to fall before a throne. There is mention of a vision. The fragmentary text continues with references to affliction and carnage and mentions "the king of Assyria and [E]gypt."

The second column is fully preserved. It speaks of someone who will be called "Son of God" and "Son of the Most High." There will be a period of tumult "until the people of God arises" and all rest from the sword. Then there will be an everlasting kingdom.

There has been a lively debate as to whether the figure called "Son of God" is a negative figure or a positive one, allied with the people of God. There is a lacuna before the phrase "until the people of God arises," and this has led some scholars to assume that the "Son of God" belongs to the time of distress and so must be a negative, evil figure.[42] But by far the closest parallel to the titles in question is explicitly messianic.[43] In Luke 1:32, the angel Gabriel tells Mary that her child:

> will be great, and will be called the Son of the Most High, and the Lord God will give to him the throne of his ancestor David. He will reign over the house of Jacob forever, and of his kingdom there will be no end.

In 1:35 he adds: "he will be called the Son of God." The Greek titles "Son of the Most High" and "Son of God" correspond exactly to the Aramaic fragment from Qumran. Both texts refer to an everlasting kingdom. Luke would not have used the Palestinian-Jewish titles with reference to the messiah if they were associated negatively with a Syrian king. The basis for referring to the messiah as Son of God is clear, not only in Ps 2 but also in 2 Sam 7 and in the *Florilegium* from Qumran. The role of the Son of God conforms to the traditional role of the messiah—to impose peace on earth by the power of God.

4Q521 speaks of a messiah whom heaven and earth will obey. It goes on to say that "the glorious things that have not taken place, the Lord will do as he said, for he will heal the wounded, give life to the dead and preach good news to the poor." These are works of the Lord, but preaching good news is usually the work of a herald or messenger (*měbaśśēr*). In Matt 11:2–6 the same works are attributed to the messiah. It also is likely that in 4Q521, the messiah whom heaven and earth obey is the agent through whom the Lord acts. If so, the messiah is here depicted as an Elijah-like figure and should be identified as a prophetic rather than a royal messiah.[44] An eschatological herald or messenger (cf. Isa 52:7) also plays a part in 11QMelch.

4Q541 is a very fragmented Aramaic text that speaks of a figure who "will atone for all the children of his people." He is a teacher, and "his light will be kindled in all the corners of the earth, and it will shine on the darkness." This figure will nonetheless encounter difficulties. "They will speak many words against him, and they will invent many . . . fictions against him and speak shameful things about him." It has been argued that this passage concerns a "suffering servant" modeled on Isa 53.[45] He is not called a messiah, but the spread of his light might be taken to have eschatological significance. The motif is paralleled in a poem about an eschatological priest in *T. Levi* 18. Since the figure in 4Q541 atones for his people, he is presumably a priest and atones by offering the prescribed sacrifices (priests were also teachers). There is no indication that his suffering was thought to have atoning significance. The abuse he encounters is similar to the opposition to the Teacher, as reflected in the *Hodayot*.[46]

There is very little evidence for Isa 53 as a messianic prophecy in pre-Christian Judaism, but there was a possible textual basis for such an interpretation. In Isa 52:14, the passage "so his appearance was destroyed [*mišḥat*] beyond that of a man" is read as "so I have anointed [*māšaḥti*] [his appearance beyond that of a man]" in the great Isaiah scroll from Qumran (1QIsaᵃ). This may be a scribal error, but it lent itself to a messianic interpretation, especially in light of Isa 61, where the prophet says that God has anointed him. Whether the text was read this way at Qumran is an open question. There are many allusions to Isa 53 in the *Hodayot*, and it is arguable that the Teacher understood himself as the suffering servant.[47] There is no good evidence, however, that the Teacher was ever regarded as a messiah.

Messiah and Son of Man

In Dan 7 "one like a son of man" appears on the clouds and is given a kingdom on behalf of "the people of the holy ones of the Most High." He appears in contrast to four beasts that symbolize four kingdoms. In the context of Daniel, this figure is not the messiah, but rather the patron angel of Israel, Michael (cf. Dan 10:21; 12:1).[48] By the first century CE, however, the two figures were associated.[49]

The Similitudes of Enoch (*1 En.* 37–71) most probably was written in the early or mid-first century CE. It has not been found in the Dead Sea Scrolls. It describes three visions of Enoch. In one of these, he sees "one who had a head of days, and his head was like white wool. And with him was another, whose face was like the appearance of a man; and his face was full of graciousness like one of the holy angels" (*1 En.* 46:1). These are evidently the same as the figures seen by Daniel. The "Son of Man" is an angelic figure although he is distinguished from Michael in this text. We are told that "his name was named" even before the sun and the constellations were created. Later, he sits as judge on the throne of glory. In two passages, 48:10 and 52:4, he is referred to as "his Anointed One" or Messiah. At the end of the Similitudes, Enoch is taken up to heaven and in chapter 71, in what appears to be a secondary appendix, he is greeted as "Son of Man." Whether, or in what sense, he is identified with the Son of Man of his visions is disputed.[50] Up to that point, there is no indication that the Son of Man ever had an earthly career. Although he is called Messiah, he is not associated with the line of David. We already have seen that the term "messiah" was not restricted to the Davidic king but also could be applied to a future priest and perhaps also to a prophet. The Similitudes illustrate another usage with reference to a heavenly, angelic figure. A similar figure is described in 11QMelch, where he is given the name of the ancient priest-king of Salem (Gen 14, cf. Ps. 110), but is described as an *ʾĕlōhîm* (divine or angelic being) who executes the judgments of God.[51] Melchizedek is not called "messiah."

Imagery associated with the Son of Man is used in connection with the Davidic messiah in *4 Ezra*, an apocalypse from the end of the first century CE that survives in Latin and other versions.[52] There, Ezra is told that "my son the Messiah shall be revealed with those who are with him, and those who remain shall rejoice four hundred years. And after these years my son the Messiah shall die and all who draw human breath" (*4 Ezra* 7:28–29). Then the world will be returned to primeval silence for seven days, after which the resurrection will follow. The messiah is not killed but apparently dies of natural causes. The roughly contemporary apocalypse of *2 (Syriac) Baruch* says that "when the time of the presence of the Messiah has run its course . . . he will return in glory," presumably to heaven. Then the resurrection will follow (*2 Bar.* 30:1). The four-hundred-year reign, like the millennium in the Book of Revelation, provides for an era of earthly fulfillment in line with traditional Old Testament expectation, before the end of the world and new creation that is characteristic of apocalyptic literature.

In *4 Ezra* 11–12, the visionary sees an eagle come up out of the sea, which is then confronted by a lion. He is told that the eagle "is the fourth kingdom which appeared in a vision to your brother Daniel, but it was not explained to

him as I now explain . . . it to you" (12:11–12). The eagle
obviously symbolizes Rome. The lion is identified as "the
Messiah whom the Most High has kept until the end of
days, who will arise from the posterity of David" (12:32). In
chapter 13, Ezra sees "something like the figure of a man"
come up from the sea and fly with the clouds. He takes his
stand on a mountain and destroys the nations who attack
him with the breath of his lips. He is identified as "my son,"
whom the Most High has been keeping for many ages, and
the mountain is identified as Mount Zion. While the
imagery of riding on the clouds recalls the "Son of Man,"
the stand on Mt. Zion and the fiery breath are clearly messianic images (cf. Ps 2, Isa 11).[53] Although the messiah is
said to be from the posterity of David, he is also said to be
a preexistent figure, like the Son of Man in the Similitudes,
whom the Lord has been keeping for many ages. The messiah also is said to be preexistent in the LXX translation of
Ps 110 (109 in Greek), where he is said to have been begotten "before the Day Star" (the Hebrew has "from dawn").[54]

The idea of a savior figure who comes from heaven also
is found in the fifth book of *Sibylline Oracles,* composed in
Egypt in the early second century CE.[55] He is variously
described as "a king sent from God" (5:108–109), an "excep-
tional man from the sky" (5:256), or "a blessed man from
the expanses of heaven with a scepter in his hands which
God gave him" (5:414). Although he is not said to be
anointed, as an eschatological king sent by God, he is
clearly a messianic figure. His heavenly origin recalls the
"Son of Man,"[56] but the language is not especially close to
that of Daniel. It is apparent in any case that the figure of
the messiah had taken on a supernatural character by the
late first and early second century CE.

Messianic Pretenders

More traditional ideas of a human, warrior messiah also
continued to flourish. Josephus reports a series of royal pre-

tenders in the first century CE, beginning after the death of Herod with Judas, whose father had been killed by Herod; Simon, a servant of Herod of imposing size; and Athronges, another person distinguished by size (*A.J.* 17.271–285).[57] We know little about these people apart from the unsympathetic account of Josephus. Josephus (*B.J.* 6.312–313) also claims that messianic expectation was a significant factor in the outbreak of the revolt against Rome in 66 CE:

> What more than all else incited them to the war was an ambiguous oracle, likewise found in their sacred scriptures, to the effect that at that time one from their country would become ruler of the world. This they understood to mean someone of their own race, and many of their wise men went astray in their interpretation of it.

Josephus held that the oracle really referred to Vespasian, who was proclaimed emperor while in Judea. Josephus portrays two of the rebel leaders as royal pretenders: Menahem, son of Judas the Galilean (*B.J.* 2.433–434), and Simon bar Giora (*B.J.* 4.503). The latter was ceremonially executed in Rome as the leader of the defeated Judeans.[58] In 115–117 CE, a revolt swept the Diaspora in Cyrene and Egypt, which was led by a messianic pretender whose name is variously give as Lukuas or Alexander (Eusebius, *Hist. eccl.* 4.2.1–5; Cassius Dio 68.32.1–3).[59] Simon Bar Kosiba, known as Bar Kochba, who led the last Jewish revolt against Rome in 132–135 CE, was allegedly hailed as messiah by Rabbi Akiba.[60] Coins from the revolt refer to him as "prince" (*nāśîʾ*), which we have seen as a messianic title in the Dead Sea Scrolls and sometimes mention him with the High Priest Eleazar.

Conclusion

Jewish messianic expectation was never uniform. The hope for the restoration of Davidic kingship was standard, but it is impossible to say how active or important it was at any given time. Moreover, the Davidic genealogy of the future king could be construed broadly, as we have seen in the case of *4 Ezra*. There was a trend toward ascribing to the royal messiah a supernatural character, but this was not universally followed. Rather, later Jewish tradition insists on his humanity. Expectations for an eschatological priest or prophet appear occasionally but were never as central as the hope for a "King Messiah."

The failure of the revolts against Rome, and of the supposedly messianic figures who led them, led to a decline in messianic fervor in the second century CE. The Mishnah only twice makes passing reference to "the days of the messiah" (*m. Ber.* 1:5 and *m. Soṭah* 9:15).[61] However, ongoing messianic hope is attested in the Jewish daily prayer, the "Eighteen Benedictions," which prays explicitly for the restoration of the throne of David and for the coming of the branch of David and also in the Aramaic biblical paraphrases, the Targums.[62] The picture of the messiah in these sources is in line with what we see in the Dead Sea Scrolls. *Targum Pseudo-Jonathan* on Genesis 49 speaks of the King Messiah girding his loins for battle and reddening the mountains with the blood of the slain. Expectation of the Davidic messiah is well attested in the Talmud (e.g. *b. Sanh.* 98a–99a).[63]

2

THE MESSIAH AS SON OF GOD IN THE SYNOPTIC GOSPELS

Adela Yarbro Collins

The Synoptic Gospels present Jesus emphatically as the Messiah of Israel, although the character and work of the holder of that office are reinterpreted in relation to Jewish texts from the Second Temple period. These Gospels associate messiahship with divine sonship. The significance of the epithet "son of God," however, is subtle and ambiguous. This essay will attempt to clarify the relation of the two epithets and their significance in Mark, Matthew, and Luke.

The Gospel according to Mark

Mark's Gospel opens with the words "The beginning of the good news of Jesus Christ." Some, but not all, manuscripts add the words "son of God." It is unlikely that an accidental omission would occur at the beginning of a work. Further, it is far easier to explain the deliberate addition of the phrase "son of God" than its omission. It may have been added out of piety or to combat an understanding of Jesus that was too human.[1]

The phrase "Jesus Christ" appears to be a proper name. However, the Greek word translated as "Christ" also may be rendered as "anointed one" or "Messiah." The same word is used with the article in Peter's statement in Mark 8:29. That acclamation should be translated "You are the Messiah." That passage, as well as others in Mark, make clear that the name or epithet "Christ" had not lost its messianic connotations for the evangelist and his early audiences.

In the account of the baptism of Jesus (Mark 1:9–11), his messiahship and divine sonship are strongly implied:

> And in those days, Jesus came from Nazareth in Galilee and was baptized in the Jordan by John. And immediately, while he was coming up out of the water, he saw the heavens split and the spirit coming down to him like a dove. And a voice came from the heavens, 'You are my beloved son; I take delight [*eudokēsa*] in you.'[2]

The voice from heaven indicates the significance of the descent of the spirit. The first part of the saying is an actualization of verse seven of Ps 2, a royal psalm in which the Lord says to the king of Israel, his anointed, "You are my son." The descent of the spirit makes it likely that God establishes Jesus as his "son" with these words. The allusion to Ps 2 implies that God thus appoints Jesus as Messiah at the time of his baptism by John. The other passage actualized in the speech of the divine voice is Isa 42:1, which reads, "Behold my servant, whom I uphold, my chosen, in whom my soul delights."

The combination of Ps 2 and Isa 42 implies that Jesus is both the Messiah and the servant of the Lord. The reason may be that the author of Mark, and perhaps his predecessors as well, read at least some of the poems about the servant of the Lord in Isaiah as messianic. The striking similarities between the fate of the servant as described in Isa 53, on the one hand, and the fate of Jesus as interpreted by some of his followers, on the other, may have been the impetus for the messianic interpretation of these poems. An effect of this combination is that the messiahship of Jesus is not presented in royal and military terms; instead the idea of the messiah of Israel is reinterpreted in prophetic terms.

Jesus is also presented as the son of God in the summary of his activities in Mark 3:7–12. A great multitude is following Jesus because he had healed many, and all who had diseases pressed upon him to touch him. "And the unclean spirits, whenever they saw him, would fall down before him and cry out, saying, 'You are the son of God!'" Jesus rebukes them "in order that they not make him known." The words of the spirits and the rebuke of Jesus suggest that they have special knowledge, concealed from the human beings who surround Jesus.

The allusion to the special knowledge of the unclean spirits, the acclamation of Jesus as "the son of God," and his rebuke of the spirits are all related to an important theme in the Gospel of Mark, the question of the identity of Jesus, often described as the "messianic secret." The first time Jesus is described as son of God in Mark, at his baptism, Jesus is the only character within the narrative who hears the divine voice. In chapter 3, it is only the unclean spirits who know Jesus' identity. These features of the narrative call the attention of the audience to Jesus' identity as son of God and lead the audience to ponder its meaning. The expression "son of God" can be linked with the Davidic messiah, since it is a prominent epithet of the king in scripture. There is evidence that the king of Israel was thought to be divine. Even if this tradition had been forgotten by the time of Mark, the role of Messiah was linked with divine

authority, since he would be God's agent. From the perspective of traditional Greek religion, the term "son of God"
implies divinity or at least heroic status.

   As indicated earlier, a very important passage for the
development of the theme of "Jesus as Messiah" in Mark
(8:27–30) is the scene in which Peter declares, "You are the
Messiah." It is clear from the context that the Davidic Messiah or royal Messiah is meant here, because the acclamation is offered as an alternative to the opinion of some that
Jesus is "one of the prophets." The response of Jesus makes
clear that the acclamation is accepted; the immediate
response is not to reject or reinterpret, but to command the
disciples to keep the identity of Jesus secret.

   The reinterpretation comes in the next, closely related
scene. Jesus speaks about the suffering, death, and resurrection of the Son of Man. Evidently, Jesus and the disciples,
as characters in the narrative, on the one hand, and the
author of Mark and his audience on the other, have a
shared understanding of the notion of the Davidic Messiah
and a shared assumption that "the Messiah" and "the Son
of Man" are equivalent. That such information is commonly
understood is clear from the fact that the use of the epithet
"Son of Man" as equivalent to "Messiah" needs no comment, explanation, or defense.[3]

   The important point is that the speech of Jesus following
the command to secrecy introduces new and controversial
information: that the Messiah must suffer, be rejected, be
killed, and rise again. Suffering, rejection, and death were
not part of the traditional picture of the role of the Messiah
of Israel. But suffering, rejection, and even death were typically associated with the prophetic role.[4] The combination
of these prophetic motifs with the royal messianic role was
very unusual in the time of Mark. That this was so is indicated by the reaction of Peter and by Jesus' strong correc-
tion of his attitude (Mark 8:32–33).

   After the teaching on discipleship that follows Peter's

acclamation and the first passion prediction, Jesus takes Peter, James, and John to a high mountain where they can be alone. In their presence he is transformed, and his clothes become very white and shining (Mark 9:2–3). Then the three disciples see Elijah and Moses conversing with Jesus. After Peter suggests that the disciples make three tents, a cloud covers them, and a voice speaks from the cloud, "This is my beloved son; listen to him" (Mark 9:7).

The motif of secrecy is implicit here, as in the summary of chapter 3, because Jesus allowed only three disciples to share in this experience. Once again the idea that Jesus is the son of God is shrouded in secrecy. The context suggests a reason for that. The messiahship of Jesus was just affirmed, again secretly, to the disciples only. This affirmation is followed by a prediction of the suffering, death, and resurrection of Jesus. The whole complex, from the discussion of Jesus' identity to the end of the transfiguration, suggests that the heart of Jesus' teaching, the message to which the disciples should listen, is that the Messiah, the son of God, must suffer.

At the same time, the account of the transfiguration suggests that Jesus is a divine being walking the earth. Although the portrayal of the baptism seems to indicate that Jesus was chosen as Messiah on that occasion, certain features of the transfiguration suggest that it is the self-manifestation of a deity.[5] Similarly, the motif of secrecy in Mark has an affinity with the notion of a deity disguising him- or herself as a human being. From the point of view of traditional Greek religion, the identification of Jesus in this scene as God's son is equivalent to identifying him as a divine being.[6]

The account of the transfiguration, read in the traditional Greek way, is in tension with the description of the baptism. This tension is resolved for later Christian readers by the assumption that Mark presupposed the preexistence and incarnation of Jesus, even though he does not mention such things. For the author and earliest audiences of Mark, the tension may have been resolved by the assumption that the transfiguration is a preview of the resurrection of Jesus. In the first century CE, not only Elijah, but also Moses, was believed to have been taken up to heaven in bodily form.[7] Similarly, after his death, Jesus would be raised from the dead and exalted to heaven.

In Mark 11:1–10, Jesus enters the city of Jerusalem in a way that suggests the fulfillment of Zech 9:9–10, understood as a messianic prophecy. The people acclaim Jesus as "the coming one" and associate him with the kingdom of their father, David.

The passion narrative of Mark is full of ironic affirmations of the kingship of Jesus. The anonymous woman in 14:3–9 is culturally an unlikely choice for the role of choosing and anointing Jesus as king, but her action suggests that such is what she is doing: she pours a bottle of aromatic oil upon his head.[8] Yet Jesus reinterprets the gesture as anointing for burial; this reinterpretation contributes to the author's redefinition of messiahship.

In one scene of the passion narrative (Mark 14:53–65), the kingship of Jesus is directly affirmed in a non-ironic way. The high priest asks him, "Are you the Messiah, the son of the Blessed?" Jesus responds, "I am; and you will see the Son of Man sitting on the right hand of the Power, and coming with the clouds of heaven" (Mark 14:62). The relation between the question and the answer, especially the opening statement, "I am," shows clearly the equivalence of "Messiah" and "Son of Man" for the author of Mark and the assumption that the audience would understand and accept it. This passage also makes clear that the rejection and suffering of Jesus belong to the period in which he is the hidden Son of Man[9] and that his exercise of the messianic office will commence after his resurrection and exaltation.

The interrogation of Jesus by Pilate forms a transition from Jesus' direct affirmation of his messiahship to the renewed irony that characterizes the final stage of the hiddenness of the Son of Man. Pilate asks him, "Are you the king of the Jews?" Jesus' response, "You say (so)," is not a denial, but it is evasive and noninformative. The irony appears in full strength in the scene in which the crowd rejects the nonviolent Jesus for the rebel Barabbas (Mark 15:6–15). It is present in powerful and poignant form in the mocking of Jesus as king by the Roman soldiers (Mark 15:16–20); in the inscription of the charge against him, "the king of the Jews" (Mark 15:26); and in the mockery of the passers-by (Mark 15:32).

The irony is shattered by the splitting of the temple veil and by the acclamation of the centurion, "This man really was God's son" (Mark 15:38–39).[10] Just as it is not entirely clear how Peter came to the insight that Jesus is the Messiah, so the reason for the centurion's affirmation in the narrative logic of the scene is somewhat obscure. Nevertheless, the link between the affirmation and the death of Jesus is unmistakable. This scene is, therefore, the climax of the reinterpretation of the traditional understanding of the royal Messiah by the author of Mark.

The splitting of the temple veil recalls the baptism, when the heavens were split. At the baptism God is present and speaks. At the cross God seems to be absent and is silent. But the splitting of the temple veil may be interpreted as a mysterious self-manifestation of God, indicating that in the death of Jesus, the will of the hidden God is manifested.

The denouement comes in the last chapter of Mark (16:1–8). The author, building upon earlier tradition, innovates in his portrayal of Jesus as messiah by including a narrative concerning the resurrection of the messiah from the dead. In an analogous way, the authors of the Similitudes of Enoch and *4 Ezra*, in large part through their appropriation of Dan 7, transformed the expectation of a royal Messiah, who would be primarily a warrior and a king, into belief in an exalted, heavenly Messiah, whose role would be to execute judgment and to inaugurate a new age of peace and rejoicing.[11]

The Gospel according to Matthew

Matthew's Gospel begins with a titular sentence similar to Mark's: "[The] account of [the] descent of Jesus Christ, son of David, son of Abraham" (Matt 1:1).

It is interesting that Matthew elaborates Mark's reference to "Jesus Christ," not with "son of God," but with "son of David, son of Abraham." The phrase "son of David" makes clear that Matthew understood the epithet "Christ" to mean "Messiah of Israel."

The idea that Jesus is the son of God is expressed indirectly in the narrative about the virginal conception of Jesus by Mary (Matt 1:18–25). The narrator informs the audience that the pregnancy is "from *a* holy spirit" or "from [*the*] holy spirit," that is, the spirit of God.[12] In either case, the idea would seem to be that the spirit in question is the efficient cause employed by God, the actual agent, in bringing about the pregnancy of a virgin.[13]

Later in this passage, the narrator comments in the first of a number of fulfillment quotations in Matthew: "All this happened in order that what was said by the Lord through the prophet might be fulfilled, saying, 'Behold, the virgin will conceive and will bear a son, and they will call his name Emmanuel'" (Matt 1:22–23).

The text cited is Isa 7:14. It has been pointed out that the Old Greek translation "probably means only that she who is now a virgin will later conceive and give birth; no miracle is involved."[14] Therefore, "the Isaian prophecy did not give rise either to the idea of the virginal conception or to Matthew's narrative."[15] What then was the catalyst that evoked a miraculous reading of Isa 7:14?[16]

The best explanation is that the author of Matthew and his predecessors were aware of Greek and Roman stories about great men being fathered by deities with human women.[17] The Isaian prophecy enabled followers of Jesus to interpret the origin of Jesus as equally or even more miraculous, since his Father is not just one among many so-called gods, but the creator of all things himself.

There is no exact or even very close parallel to Matthew's story in Greek and Latin literature for two reasons. First, the story is analogous to and probably inspired by Greek and Roman stories, but the typical form of the story is adapted to a Jewish context. Second, like some Greeks and others roughly contemporary with Matthew, the evangelist rejected the mythological expression of the idea. In other words, they rejected the idea that an anthropomorphic god could have relations with a human woman. Yet they believed that a divine spirit could approach a human woman and make her pregnant.[18]

The conclusion that Jesus is portrayed as God's son in this passage suggests how the name "Emmanuel" in the formula quotation should be understood.[19] Matthew explains it as meaning "God with us."[20] If Jesus is portrayed as son of God, it is too much to say that "Emmanuel" implies that Jesus is "God."[21] But it is too little to infer, as Davies and Allison do, that Jesus is a human being "in whom God's active presence, that is, the divine favor and blessing and aid, have manifested themselves."[22] As son of God, Jesus is divine, yet subordinated to God.[23] God's active presence is manifest in him, not only because he is divine, but also because he is God's appointed agent, the Messiah of Israel.

The Gospel according to Luke

Luke begins much differently from Mark and Matthew, with a formal preface that does not even mention Jesus explicitly. Jesus is introduced for the first time in the scene traditionally referred to as the Annunciation (Luke 1:26–38).

In contrast to Matthew, the angel is named rather than

unnamed and sent to Mary, rather than to Joseph. As in Matthew, Mary is identified as a virgin (*parthenos*) engaged to be married to Joseph. The angel announces to Mary (Luke 1:31–33):

> And behold, you will conceive in your womb and will bear a son and you shall call his name "Jesus." He will be great and will be called "son of the Most High" and the Lord God will give him the throne of David, his father, and he will rule over the house of Jacob forever, and of his kingdom there will be no end.

Gabriel reveals that Jesus will be both son of God and Messiah. The notion of his being son of God is formulated in terms of his being called "son of the Most High." His messiahship is expressed in the saying that God will give Jesus "the throne of David, his father." Thus Luke closely links his being "son of the Most High" with his messiahship, that is, his role as king in the restoration of the house of David and the kingdom of Israel in the last days.

The definitive and eternal character of his rule and kingdom are expressed in synonymous parallel statements: "he will rule over the house of Jacob forever, and of his kingdom there will be no end." This affirmation is probably inspired by the promise in 2 Sam 7 that God will "establish *the throne of his kingdom forever*" and that "your *house* and your *kingdom* will be made sure *forever*."[24] It also evokes the book of Daniel. When kingship is given to the one like a son of man, Daniel says: "His dominion is everlasting dominion, which will not pass away, and his kingdom is indestructible."[25]

Then Mary asks, "How will this be?" and Gabriel replies: "[The] holy spirit will come upon you, and [the] power of [the] Most High will overshadow you; therefore, the child to be born will be called holy, son of God" (Luke 1:35).[26] The conception is brought about by the holy spirit coming upon Mary and by the power of the Most High overshadowing her. The parallel expressions may be read as implying that the holy spirit is equivalent to "the power of God" and thus the efficient cause of the conception. The answer to Mary's question is therefore similar to the account in Matthew: God is the ultimate agent of the conception, so that God may be called the father of the child.

Luke's narrative does not speak of God in an anthropomorphic or mythological way. The event is described in an elevated and subtle manner. Nevertheless, the scene evokes the myths and legends of the births of famous Greek and Roman men.[27] As in Matthew, the narrative about the virginal conception of Jesus in Luke implies that he is divine. In both Gospels, Jesus is "son of God" in a stronger sense than in Mark. The narratives in Matthew and Luke do not imply preexistence, but the notion of virginal conception was easily combined with ideas about preexistence and incarnation later on.

Results

The portrayal of Jesus as son of God in Mark is ambiguous. It may be read as implying that Jesus was an ordinary human being whose powers of healing and teaching were due to his possession of the holy spirit of God during his earthly activity. After his death, he became divine in the sense of sharing in the immortal nature of God and in the authority of God to rule all creation. Or Mark may be read as presupposing the preexistence of Jesus as a divine being.

Matthew and Luke, apparently independently, portrayed Jesus as son of God in a stronger sense. He had no human father, but was miraculously conceived by the holy spirit of God. Those Gospels also are open to a variety of readings. The Christian churches have combined the virginal conception with the idea of the incarnation. The Koran accepts the claim that a virgin conceived Jesus. It interprets this event, however, as less remarkable than the creation of Adam apart from any father or mother.

Among the Gospels, it is only in John that the idea of incarnation is explicitly expressed. The controversies concerning the nature of Jesus from the second to the fourth centuries show, however, that even John did not yet express clearly what came to be the official definition of the incarnation.

3

Paul and the Missing Messiah[1]

Magnus Zetterholm

The Problem

When it comes to the figure of Jesus, there are some very striking differences between the Gospels and the letters of Paul. The Gospels, which were written between 70 and 100 CE, focus almost entirely on Jesus' earthly ministry and clearly are trying to present Jesus in his historical context. The authors of the Gospels present us with the *story* of Jesus—his various deeds and basic teaching—culminating in the narratives of his suffering, death, and resurrection. This is theologized history, but history nevertheless.[2] In the introduction to Luke's Gospel, the author specifically mentions his intention to write a historical account of Jesus' life and deeds (Luke 1:1–4):

> Since many have undertaken to set down an orderly account of the events that have been fulfilled among us, just as they were handed on to us by those who from the beginning were eyewitnesses and servants

of the word, I too decided, after investigating everything carefully from the very first, to write an orderly
account for you, most excellent Theophilus, so that
you may know the truth concerning the things about
which you have been instructed.[3]

Paul, on the other hand, wrote his letters fifteen to twenty
years *before* the first gospel, Mark, was written down and
seems rather uninterested in the earthly ministry of Jesus.
His letters reveal almost no knowledge about the historical
figure of Jesus. Paul refers only a few times to traditions
about Jesus, for instance, in 1 Cor 15:3–5 where he mentions
that Jesus "died for our sins in accordance with the scriptures, and that he was buried, and that he was raised on the
third day in accordance with the scriptures, and that he
appeared to Cephas, then to the twelve." Similarly, in 1 Cor
11:23–26, Paul describes Jesus' last supper in a similar way
to the versions that appear later in the Synoptic Gospels.[4]

Perhaps it is significant that the few instances where Paul
actually refers to the earthly Jesus, it is in connection to his
death.[5] In Paul's view, Jesus' significance lies not in his
earthly ministry but entirely in his crucifixion, resurrection,
and exaltation.[6] This is, of course, disappointing since Paul's
letters are the earliest sources we have of the early Jesus
movement. If Paul had revealed some substantial knowledge about the earthly Jesus, this would have brought us
about fifteen years closer to the real events.

The difference between the Gospels and the letters of
Paul may, of course, be a matter of genre. In fact, none of
the writings in the New Testament, apart from the Gospels,
deal in any significant way with the historical Jesus. The
authors of the Gospels were involved in a process of transmitting (and reworking) traditions about Jesus, while Paul
wrote letters to various communities, mainly to deal with
local problems. It is, of course, possible that Paul passed on
traditions of the life and teaching of Jesus when he visited

the communities. However, Paul also was involved in a process of transmitting some traditions as is explicitly stated in, for instance, 1 Cor 11:2 ("remember me in everything and maintain the traditions just as I handed them on to you"), 1 Cor 11:23 ("I received from the Lord what I also handed on to you"), and 1 Cor 15:3 ("I handed on to you as of first importance what I in turn had received: that Christ died for our sins in accordance with the scriptures").[7]

The differences between the presentation of Jesus in the Gospels and in Paul are too profound to be explained away only as a matter of different genres. The Gospels create the impression that the identity of Jesus was an important issue during his lifetime. The Synoptic Gospels have, in slightly different ways, preserved the story of Peter's confession (Mark 8:27–30; Matt 16:13–20; Luke 9:18–21). The account begins with a question from Jesus who is trying to find out what people say about him. In Mark's version, Jesus asks: "Who do people say that I am?" (8:27). Mark reports that people claim that Jesus is John the Baptist, Elijah, or "one of the prophets" (8:28). In Matthew's version (16:14), people specifically mention the prophet Jeremiah, and according to Luke (9:19), people believe that "one of the ancient prophets" may have arisen or that Jesus is John the Baptist or Elijah.

When the disciples are asked the same question, Peter asserts that Jesus is "the Messiah" (*ho christos*) (Mark 8:29). *Christos* is the Greek translation of the Hebrew word *māšîah*, which simply means "anointed one" and is used with reference to the king, the high priest, or a prophet in the Hebrew Bible.[8] Matthew adds "the Son of the living God" (Matt 16:16), and according to Luke, Peter called Jesus "the Messiah of God" (Luke 9:20). The story of Peter's confession implies that it was natural for people to identify a religious figure, such as Jesus, with ancient prophets like Elijah or Jeremiah or with some other charismatic figure. The Gospels certainly indicate that there seems to have been some discussion about who Jesus really was.[9]

In contrast to popular conceptions about Jesus, the Gospels clearly identify Jesus with the Messiah of Israel. The crowds may have believed that Jesus was a prophet, but the authors of the Gospels knew the true identity of Jesus. Mark, for instance, opens his gospel with the statement: "The beginning of the good news of Jesus Christ, [the Son of God]."[10] Even though it is possible to understand the phrase "Jesus Christ" (*Iēsou Christou*) as a proper name here,[11] there can be no doubt that Mark creates a very specific referential connection between the name "Jesus" and the idea of "the Messiah."[12] Apart from Peter's confession in Mark 8:29, which of course also serves the purpose of identifying Jesus as the Messiah, there is another, perhaps even more significant, statement in Mark 14:61–62.[13] After being arrested, Jesus is brought before the high priest who asks him: "Are you the Messiah [*ho Christos*], the Son of the Blessed One?" Jesus' answer could not be any clearer: "I am; and 'you will see the Son of Man seated at the right hand of the Power,' and 'coming with the clouds of heaven.'"[14] Thus, Mark clearly identifies Jesus as the Messiah of Israel.[15]

Of course, this statement involves an extensive redefinition of the concept of the Messiah, who was hardly expected to suffer, die, and rise again according to Jewish tradition.[16] Nevertheless, Mark indisputably makes a connection to existing messianic notions, at least implicitly,[17] but these are transformed and filled in part with new content. Yet, there can be no doubt that Mark aims at presenting Jesus as the Messiah of Israel. The same also is true for the other canonical Gospels. Jesus is called "the Messiah," "the Son of the living God," "the Son of God," "the Son of Man," "the Son of David." His mighty acts and teaching are presented with the one and only purpose: "so that you may come to believe that Jesus is the Messiah [*Iēsous estin ho christos*], the Son of God, and that through believing you may have life in his name" (John 20:31).[18]

In Paul's letters, however, any tendency to stress the messiahship of Jesus has vanished into thin air. As mentioned previously, Paul shows little interest in the earthly ministry of Jesus or his teaching. But what is even more remarkable is that Paul rarely refers to Jesus as the Messiah in the way the Gospels do. For instance, the designation "Son of God," an important messianic title in the Gospels,[19] is almost exclusively used by Paul to stress Jesus' relationship with God rather than defining him as the Messiah and occurs only about fifteen times in the authentic Pauline letters.[20] To be sure, Paul frequently uses the word *christos*, "Christ," (about two hundred times), but there is almost complete unanimity among scholars that this expression has become a proper name and that it has lost its messianic overtones almost entirely.[21] For instance, Jesus is never explicitly called "the Messiah," that is, Paul never uses "Christ" as a predication of Jesus in formulations, such as "Jesus is the Christ."[22] Furthermore, the traditional messianic texts from the Hebrew Bible do not play any essential role in Paul's letters.[23]

The most important way that Paul refers to Jesus theologically is as "Lord" (*kyrios*) (about 180 times), either on its own or in different combinations: "Jesus Christ our Lord," "our Lord Jesus," or "Christ Jesus our Lord."[24] The importance of this designation for Paul can be demonstrated by the fact that in some instances, he actually seems to have inserted the designation *kyrios* in traditions he himself had received and in which *kyrios* did not originally belong. As mentioned previously, Paul states in 1 Cor 15:3 that he passes on a tradition he himself had received. Behind Paul's formulation lies what W. Kramer has called the pistis formula, a short summary of the faith and content of the preaching of the early Jesus movement that focused on "the saving acts of death and resurrection."[25] This formula, which probably stems from the Aramaic-speaking Jewish part of the Jesus movement, originally contained a statement such as "God raised Jesus" or "the

Messiah."[26] Eventually, this basic formula was developed into the four-part formula we find in 1 Cor 15:3–5.

After analyzing all possible allusions to the *pistis* formula in its different stages of development in the New Testament, Kramer arrives at the conclusion that "Lord" (*kyrios*) was never part of the original *pistis* formula,[27] which probably used "Christ" or "Jesus." In most instances, Paul kept these original designations, but in some texts, it is evident that he has modified the tradition he received and used the title "Lord" (*kyrios*) instead. Thus, in 1 Cor 6:14, Paul states that "God raised the Lord [*ton kyrion*]," and in 2 Cor 4:14, he proclaims that "we know that the one who raised the Lord Jesus [*ton kyrion Iēsoun*] will raise us also with Jesus." In Rom 4:24, he asserts that Abraham's righteousness will be reckoned to them "who believe in him who raised Jesus our Lord [*Iēsoun ton kyrion hēmōn*] from the dead."

Since these texts speak against Kramer's overarching thesis that "Lord" was not part of the original pistis formula, he is anxious to find reasonable explanations as to why they appear in contexts where, according to him, they should not. Hence, regarding 1 Cor 6:14 and Rom 4:24, he claims that Paul is responsible for having modified the tradition.[28] As for 2 Cor 4:14, he refers to the fact that there is some text-critical ambiguity concerning the exact wording. In some important manuscripts, the word "Lord" is missing. Thus, according to $\mathfrak{p}^{46}$ (an early papyrus, ca 200) and B (Codex Vaticanus, fourth century), Paul only mentioned "Jesus," as in the original *pistis* formula. However, the relevant early codices, some early translations, and the Majority Text all support the reading that includes "Lord."[29] If we take into account that Paul seems to be responsible for having exchanged "Jesus," or perhaps "Christ," for "Lord" in 1 Cor 6:14 and in Rom 4:24, the text-critical doubts raised by $\mathfrak{p}^{46}$ and B seem less weighty. Thus, it seems safe to conclude that Paul deliberately changed the wording in all these texts.

Irrespective of the precise background for the use of "Lord" as referring to Jesus within the early Jesus movement,[30] is seems clear that it predates Paul and that its original setting was confined to the context of worship.[31] To some extent, Paul's use of the designation reflects this original stage,[32] but at the same time, *he also creatively extends the use of this specific title within his particular theological framework.* Kramer concludes: "Paul uses the title [*kyrios*] with greater emphasis, to qualify the 'secular activities' of daily life."[33]

Paul's use of the designations "Christ" and "Lord" makes it clear that his fundamental confession was not, as Peter's was, "Jesus is the Messiah," but "Jesus is Lord."[34] The hymn in Phil 2:5–11 (which probably also belongs to a pre-Pauline tradition)[35] summarizes his view of Jesus quite well:

> Let the same mind be in you that was in Christ Jesus, who, though he was in the form of God, did not regard equality with God as something to be exploited, but emptied himself, taking the form of a slave, being born in human likeness. And being found in human form, he humbled himself and became obedient to the point of death—even death on a cross. Therefore God also highly exalted him and gave him the name that is above every name, so that at the name of Jesus every knee should bend, in heaven and on earth and under the earth, and every tongue should confess that Jesus Christ is Lord to the glory of God the Father.

In Paul's letters, we find no evidence of any confusion regarding Jesus' identity but rather a homogeneous, well-defined picture of God's loyal servant, the exalted Lord of heaven and earth. Even though Paul certainly believed that Jesus was the Messiah of Israel,[36] we must conclude that he did not emphasize this aspect, and there can be little doubt that he presents Jesus in a way that differs significantly from the Gospels. In short, the messiahship of Jesus is in no way stressed in Paul's letters.[37]

Scholars often explain this by referring to Paul's specific communication situation. Since Paul directed his message predominantly to non-Jews, he had to use concepts that were intelligible to a non-Jewish audience. Non-Jews are assumed to have lacked knowledge about the cultural codes that would have made it possible for them to understand the Jewish concept of the Messiah.[38] Consequently, Paul made use of and also developed a Christology that made sense in a predominantly non-Jewish environment.

There is, in my view, some truth in this, but I would nevertheless like to suggest an important change of perspective. I would assume that Paul adapted his message about Jesus for a non-Jewish audience not because of their lack of familiarity with Jewish traditions, but rather because in Paul's view, non-Jewish believers in Jesus *were too involved with Jewish traditions*. Paul's de-emphasizing of Jesus' messiahship, while stressing his lordship, was a result of the fact that non-Jewish adherents to the Jesus movement *were already familiar with Judaism, and partly identified themselves with the salvation history of the Jewish people in which the Messiah of Israel had a key role*. I believe this is the fundamental misunderstanding of the non-Jews that Paul is generally trying to correct, and in the following sections, I will try to explain how his specific use of Christological titles fits with this overarching strategy.

Non-Jewish Involvement in Judaism

Ancient sources indicate that the Jewish communities in the large cities of the Roman Empire exercised a considerable influence on the non-Jewish population. The Jewish historian Josephus, for instance, tells us that the Jews of Antioch "were constantly attracting to their religious ceremonies multitudes of Greeks, and these they had in some measure incorporated with themselves" (*B.J.* 7.45).[39] It is not entirely clear what Josephus meant by stating that the Jews had "in some measure incorporated" non-Jews with themselves. It could mean that non-Jews had become Jews,[40] which occasionally occurred, but it is more likely that Josephus was referring to non-Jews who participated in the activities of the synagogues without converting to Judaism.[41] It seems as though this was a rather common phenomenon, and it was fully compatible with the nature of Greco-Roman religion. As long as ordinary inhabitants in cities under Roman rule fulfilled their obligations to the official religion, they were free to participate in any religious cult that was approved by the authorities.[42]

Evidently, significant groups of non-Jews were interested in Judaism and even adapted to a Jewish lifestyle. Josephus mentions this very explicitly (*C. Ap.* 2.282):

> The masses have long since shown a keen desire to adopt our religious observances; and there is not one city, Greek or barbarian, nor a single nation, to which our custom of abstaining from work on the seventh day has not spread, and where the fasts and the lighting of lamps and many of our prohibitions in the matter of food are not observed.

Josephus probably exaggerates somewhat, but Roman authors also confirm that non-Jews adopted Jewish customs. In a passage cited by Augustine (*Civ.* 6.11), Seneca expresses his concern about Romans who imitate a Jewish way of life: "the customs of this accursed race have gained such influence that they are now received throughout the world. The vanquished have given laws to their victors."[43]

It is possible that one reason why non-Jews imitated a Jewish way of life was that they were encouraged to do so by Jews who believed that the Torah was given to all mankind, not only to the Jewish people. M. Hirshman argued for the existence of a group within early Tannaitic Judaism that believed not only that the Torah was given to all peoples, but also that non-Jews could benefit from observing the Torah without becoming Jews. In *Mekilta de R. Yismael* (Bahodesh 1), in an interpretation of Exod 19:2, the midrash reads:

> *They encamped in the wilderness.* The Torah was given in public, openly in a free place. For had the Torah been given in the land of Israel, the Israelites could have said to the nations of the world: You have no share in it. But now that it was given in the wilderness publicly and openly in a place that is free for all, everyone wishing to accept it could come and accept it.[44]

According to Hirshman, this text is a "clear signal that the Torah was not the property of one nation but was intended for all people."[45] Furthermore, in *Sipra* to Lev 18:1–5, a non-Jew "doing Torah" is even compared to the high priest and involvement in the Torah, *with an emphasis on fulfilling the commandments,* is affirmed.[46] Hirshman concludes that these and other texts reveal "an effort to define Judaism as available to the non-Jew while sustaining the privileged position of the priesthood."[47] According to this non-messianic tradition within Tannaitic Judaism, non-Jews were invited to participate in Torah observance without converting to Judaism.

In a similar way, S. Stowers has drawn attention to a universalistic tendency within first-century Judaism that presented the Torah as a superior way of achieving the Greco-Roman ideal of "self-mastery" (*enkrateia*). In *Spec.* 2.61–62, for instance, Philo claims: "the law bids us take the time for studying philosophy and thereby improve the soul and the dominant mind. So each seventh day there stand wide open in every city thousands of schools of good sense, temperance, courage, justice and other virtues."[48] Stowers points out that "school" (*didaskaleion*) here should be understood as "synagogue" and that Philo states that these were open also to non-Jews since the reason for Jews to inhabit the civilized world is "that they have a mission to be to the whole world as the priest is to the whole Jewish people."[49]

According to Stowers, the reason why non-Jews were attracted to Judaism and adopted a Jewish lifestyle was precisely this interpretation of the Torah as a means to achieve self-mastery. The resemblance to the universalistic ideology within Tannaitic Judaism is striking, and it seems safe to conclude that during the first centuries of the Common Era, several sources suggest the existence of a Jewish ideology that promoted non-Jewish involvement in Torah observance without requiring conversion to Judaism. Non-Jews could continue to participate in the official religion and at the same time observe the Torah.

Thus, during the first century CE, we find a clear interest in Judaism among non-Jews who participated as guests in the synagogues of the Diaspora. Without being exclusively committed to worshipping only the God of Israel, a significant number of non-Jews were quite well informed about Jewish traditions, probably encouraged by Jews, who for different reasons believed that the Torah was meant to be observed by all people. Modern studies of religious conversion may help us confirm this conclusion.

Networks and Conversion

The classical idea of a dramatic conversion from one religion to another, as in A. D. Nock's pioneering study from 1933,[50] probably is not the most fitting conceptual role model for describing non-Jewish involvement in the Jewish communities of the Diaspora. Most non-Jews who associated themselves with the Jewish communities during antiquity had no intention of converting to Judaism. The idea of belonging to a certain religion was quite foreign to the antique world, and although religion could be connected to a certain ethnic identity,[51] this did not mean that an individual felt compelled to worship only one specific deity. Different religious manifestations existed side by side, and most Greco-Roman cults were completely compatible. There simply was no need for conversion from one religion to another as most cults were part of a common religious system.[52] However, modern approaches to religious conversion allow for broader definitions,[53] and the general mechanisms involved in the conversion process can shed light on the relation between Jews and non–Jews during antiquity.

One of the most important aspects of religious conversion is the relevance of interpersonal attachments. The sociologist R. Stark has suggested the following proposition about religious conversions: *"Conversion to new, deviant religious groups occurs when, other things being equal, people have or develop stronger attachments to members of the group than they have to nonmembers."*[54] In the initial phase, it seems as if interpersonal attachments are even more important than the ideological content of the new faith. Furthermore, there is a strong tendency among new converts to conform to the *behavior* in the new group. Stark states: "conversion is not about seeking or embracing an ideology; it is about bringing one's religious behavior into alignment with that of one's friends and family members."[55] Hence, modern data suggest that new religions typically spread through existing social networks and depend on interpersonal attachments. In addition, new converts are prone to conform to the religious *behavior* of the new faith.

Stark also points out that founders of new religious movements usually first turn to those with whom they already have strong interpersonal attachments.[56] Moreover, in addition to networks and personal attachments, familiarity with the new religion is of great importance. Stark points out that people *"are more willing to adopt a new religion to the extent that it retains cultural continuity with religion(s) with which they already are familiar."*[57]

Therefore, it is sociologically most likely that the majority of non-Jews who were recruited to the Jesus movement came from this group of non-Jews who had previously been in contact with Judaism. These non-Jews had developed interpersonal attachments with Jews, they had adopted Jewish religious customs, and they probably were also rather well informed of the ideological background of Jewish traditions. According to Augustine, Seneca stated that Jews, in general, were "aware of the origin and meaning of their rites," while "the greater part of the people go through a ritual not knowing why they do so" (*Civ.* 6.11). This general ideological awareness within the Jewish community likely affected those non-Jews who participated in the activities of synagogues. Consequently, when Acts 11:19–21 describes how Jewish believers in Jesus in Antioch first turned to Jews and then to non-Jews—who immediately responded positively to the message about Jesus—we find a strong indication that this occurred in the context of a synagogue where Jews and non-Jews previously had interacted, and where non-Jews were well informed about Jewish traditions and behavior.[58] In fact, familiarity with Jewish traditions and interpersonal attachments were necessary conditions for non-Jews to accept the idea of Jesus as the Messiah of Israel.

From this perspective, the ancient data appear in a new light, because this means that non-Jewish believers in Jesus probably had a rather profound knowledge of Jewish traditions and shared Jewish cultural codes to such an extent that they understood very well the concept of the Messiah. If this is true, there must be a reason for Paul's presentation of Jesus other than as an adaptation to a non-Jewish context where Jesus-as-the-Messiah-of-Israel meant virtually nothing. To understand why Paul downplayed Jesus'

messiahship, we must instead turn to one of the most complex issues in New Testament scholarship: Paul's view of the Torah.

Paul and the Torah

Traditionally, Paul is pictured as the one who liberated Christianity from the burden of Judaism. Paul is assumed to have rejected the possibility that the Torah could make a human being righteous in the eyes of God and is usually thought to have made a radical break with Judaism.[59] In Christian theology, the absolute contrast between Judaism and Christianity has been one of the most important cornerstones since Christianity emerged as a non-Jewish religion in the beginning of the second century. Judaism was pictured as an inferior, even perverted religion, in which the individual strove to become accepted by performing empty rituals and by following the obsolete regulations of the Torah.[60] During the nineteenth and twentieth centuries, this theologically motivated contrast between Judaism and Christianity also became the normal assumption in the majority of New Testament scholarship.

More recent scholarship has rightly unveiled the confessional component in the traditional paradigm and presented a completely different picture of ancient Judaism. Today, it is generally acknowledged that first-century Judaism was a living, dynamic religion, in which Torah observance was related to the idea that the God of Israel had entered into a covenantal relationship with the Jewish people. It was a religion that provided means for atonement of sins and for the restoration of a broken relation to God. Torah observance was not seen as a way of earning salvation but was the Jewish people's response to being made righteous through entering into a covenant with God.[61]

This new way of looking at ancient Judaism has resulted in a rather different approach to Paul. Many scholars have reached the conclusion that Paul never dealt with the way

Jewish believers in Jesus should relate to Judaism in general, or to Torah observance in particular, but exclusively discussed how non-Jewish believers in Jesus should relate to Judaism.[62] From this general assumption, I would like to suggest a somewhat novel approach to the problem of Paul's view of the Torah that, in addition, can help us understand why Paul presents Jesus the way he does.

As we noted previously, Judaism held an attraction for non-Jews. It may have been the case that Jews encouraged non-Jews to remain non-Jews but to adopt Jewish customs and to observe the Torah. There are strong indications of the existence of a universalistic tendency within first century Judaism. Although some Jewish groups may have encouraged such an ideology, there is evidence that not all Jews shared this specific form of universalism.

Early rabbinic literature shows that the idea that the Torah was to be observed by all peoples coexisted with a conflicting opinion, namely that the Torah was God's special gift to the Jewish people. A midrash (*Sipre*, pisqa 345) redacted in the late third century but containing much older traditions compares the involvement of the non-Jew in the Torah to adultery:

> [T]he Torah is betrothed to Israel and is like a married woman with respect to the nations of the world. And so it says, "Can a man rake embers into his bosom without burning his clothes? Can a man walk on live coals without scorching his feet? It is the same with one who sleeps with his fellow's wife; none who touches her will go unpunished (Prov 6:27–29).[63]

According to this view, anyone who involves himself or herself with the Torah outside a legally defined commitment is guilty of a severe sin. The Torah is certainly for all Israel, but *only* for Israel, and the fire metaphor further emphasizes the view of Torah as the exclusive property of Israel.[64]

The same idea is conveyed in a text from the Mishnah (*m. ʾAbot* 3:14):

> He [Rabbi Akiva] used to say: Beloved is man [*ʾādām*], for he was created in the image (of God); still greater was this love in that it was made known to him that he was created in the image (of God), as it is written (*Gen.* 9:6): "In the image of God made He man." Beloved are Israel, for they are called children of God; still greater was his love in that it was made known to them that they are called children of God, as it is written (*Deut.* 14:1): "You are the children of the Lord your God." Beloved are Israel, for to them was given a precious instrument; still greater was his love in that it was known to them that to them was given a precious instrument with which the world was created, as it is written (*Prov.* 4:2): "For I give you good doctrine; forsake not my Torah."[65]

According to this text, all mankind (*ʾādām*) was created in the image of God but only the people of Israel are called the "children of God" and only the people of Israel were given the Torah.[66]

Did this idea also exist during the first century? If we assume that Paul's implied audience was non-Jewish, his statements with regard to the Torah may, in fact, be taken as evidence for the existence of an ideology that opposed non-Jewish involvement in the Torah as early as the first century. Such a conclusion makes way for a radically new perspective on Paul's view of the Torah in general, and on his downplaying of Jesus' messiahship in particular.

A Strategy for De-Judaizing Non-Jews

If we assume that non-Jews who became engaged in the Jesus movement were influenced by a Jewish ideology that favored non-Jewish involvement in the Torah and that Paul was of the opposite opinion, we would expect him to deal with this particular problem. We would find him involved in trying to influence non-Jews to stop observing the Torah and to become less ideologically attached to Judaism. In fact, from the previously stated assumptions it is fully possible to understand Paul's critique of the Torah as part of a rhetorical strategy to prevent non-Jews from observing the Torah the way Jews did. In the letters to the Romans and to the Galatians, the Torah is an important issue, and Paul seems to rule out the possibility that Torah observance results in anything positive: "'no human being will be justified in [God's] sight' by deeds prescribed by the law," Paul states in Rom 3:20. The "righteousness of God" has been disclosed "apart from the law" (Rom 3:21), "a person is justified by faith apart from works prescribed by the law" (Rom 3:28), and "we know that a person is justified not by the works of the law but through faith in Jesus Christ" (Gal 2:16).

Traditionally these and similar statements were taken as proof of Paul's repudiation of Judaism. But to correctly understand what Paul is trying to communicate, we must relate these statements to his overarching strategy: to prevent non-Jews from relying on Torah observance and to uphold the ethnic boundaries between Jews and non-Jews in the Jesus movement. It is quite evident that it was important for Paul that Jews within the Jesus movement remained Jews and that non-Jews remained non-Jews. In 1 Cor 7:17–18 Paul explicitly states that an ethnic distinction is desirable:

[L]et each of you lead the life that the Lord has assigned, to which God called you. This is my rule in all the churches. Was anyone at the time of his call already circumcised? Let him not seek to remove the marks of circumcision. Was anyone at the time of his call uncircumcised? Let him not seek circumcision.

Romans 3:28–29 may explain why this was important for Paul:

> For we hold that a person is justified by faith apart from works prescribed by the law. Or is God the God of Jews only? Is he not the God of Gentiles also? Yes, of Gentiles also, since God is one; and he will justify the circumcised on the ground of faith and the uncircumcised through that same faith.

As M. D. Nanos argued, Paul may have thought that God's "oneness" would be compromised if humanity would only consist of Jews.[67] From Paul's perspective, humanity was made up of Jews and non-Jews who were to be saved according to these categories. Non-Jews imitating Jews would consequently blur the distinction between Jew and non-Jew.

It is equally clear that Paul and the leading circles within the Jesus movement opposed non-Jewish conversions to Judaism. Evidently, the question of how Jews and non-Jews should relate to each other was a burning issue within the early Jesus movement. According to Acts 15:1, one solution was to make Jews out of the non-Jews: "Then certain individuals came down from Judea and were teaching the brothers, "Unless you are circumcised according to the custom of Moses, you cannot be saved."

From a Jewish perspective, this option seems reasonable. Even though there are Jewish texts that speak about some kind of inclusion, or even salvation, of the nations in the last days,[68] only a Jew living in a covenantal relationship with the God of Israel could be certain of having a share in the world to come.[69] It is important to notice that there is an immense difference between having social contacts with non-Jews that encourage them to participate in the wisdom of the Torah and assigning to them a specific place within the salvation history of Israel that would guarantee them a share in the salvation provided by the God of Israel. The idea that only Jews living within the covenant could be saved is therefore a quite natural standpoint.

But according to Acts, the Jerusalem conference—where the question of the status of the non-Jew was to be settled— came to a completely different resolution. In contrast to "certain individuals" (Acts 15:1) and "some believers who belonged to the sect of the Pharisees" (Acts 15:5) who wanted non-Jews to convert to Judaism, the early Jesus movement decided that non-Jews should remain non-Jews. Paul confirms this decision, too (Gal 2:1–10), and even though there seem to have been groups within the Jesus movement who disagreed with this mainstream decision, there can be little doubt that the movement, in general, opposed conversion of non-Jews.

Jesus as Lord

To present Jesus as the Messiah of Israel for judaizing non-Jews, who observed the Torah and even partly identified themselves with the Jewish people, hardly would serve the purpose of preventing them from becoming less attached to the Jewish soteriological system: Torah observance in a covenantal context. Instead that would have contributed to the continuation of the ethnic confusion that Paul is trying to correct. And since the idea that Jews and non-Jews were to be saved precisely according to these ethnic categories was of such theological, eschatological, and soteriological importance for Paul, he had to present Jesus in a way that did not jeopardize God's plan for saving the world. Even though the concept of the Messiah was largely reinterpreted within the Jesus movement, it was, of course, still completely Jewish and connected to Jewish eschatological expectations.

Instead of emphasizing the role that Jesus had in a Jewish context—as the Messiah of Israel—Paul stressed an aspect of Jesus' messiahship that would help non-Jewish believers in Jesus to focus on their own ethnic identity and social situation.[70] By emphasizing Jesus' messianic role as the exalted Lord of the universe and savior of mankind, Paul deliberately challenged the political power of Rome. As N. T. Wright argued, the primary reference to the designation "Lord" in the Greco-Roman world would be to Caesar, not to private cults or mystery religions.[71] This had a direct bearing on the situation of the non-Jewish believers in Jesus, as in this way Paul was actually encouraging Jesus-believing non-Jews to accept their ethnic identity and endure any sufferings or conflicts with the political power that might come from their involvement in the Jesus movement. And such conflicts were likely to come.

In the Roman Empire, any inhabitant of a city was expected to express loyalty to the religious-political system. Failure to fulfill the religious obligations could have severe consequences, resulting in confiscation of property or, in some cases, the death penalty.[72] Religion was in fact inseparable from what we would call civic aspects of society,[73] and from the perspective of the authorities, proper cult observation guaranteed a positive relationship with the gods.[74] During the early imperial period, the importance of religion increased. Augustus's project of restoring peace and prosperity to the empire after the civil wars resulted in the development of an imperial theology that was very much centered on the emperor. For instance, in 12 BCE Augustus was elected *pontifex maximus* and, for the first time, Roman religion had a head who controlled all religious authority.[75] Even before his death, Augustus was bestowed with honors that in practice made him very similar to a god, a status he certainly received upon his death.[76] Through the imperial cults, the gospel of Augustus was spread over the world. In the words of Crossan and Reed:

> In every city of rich Roman Asia there was decreed, for all time past, present, and future, but one over-

whelming gospel, the good news of Augustus's advent, epiphany, and presence, the good news of a global Lord, divine Son, and cosmic Savior.[77]

During the reigns of Augustus's successors, conflicts between the imperial gospel and the gospel of Jesus Christ became unavoidable, because the ideology of the early Jesus movement created a rather complicated situation for non-Jewish adherents. On the one hand, they were not to become Jews, but on the other hand, they were supposed to refrain from pagan cults, including the official religion, without having the legal protection that a Jewish identity would have provided. The Jewish communities usually were granted special permission to refrain from participation in the official religion.[78]

One may, of course, wonder to what extent non-Jewish believers in Jesus really disconnected from their original religious traditions, as it was hardly possible to participate in the normal life of Greco-Roman society without being involved in some religious activities that from a Jewish perspective would be considered "idolatry." Paul's urgent and frequent warnings of the consequences of idolatry could indicate that non-Jewish believers in Jesus may not have been inclined to readily accept the idea of completely refraining from their normal religious behavior. Paul's discussion of "food sacrificed to idols" in 1 Cor 8–10 could be understood as an attempt to define the limits of involvement in Greco-Roman cultic activities.[79] But in general, non-Jews who were connected to the Jesus movement were at the least expected to avoid participation in the official religion. Sooner or later this was likely to bring non-Jewish adherents to the Jesus movement into conflict with the political system. As Crossan and Reed stated: "Deep down beneath an Augustus or a Jesus, a Paul or a Nero, two giant tectonic plates ground relentlessly against one another in that first century."

Thus, Paul's theological convictions regarding non-Jewish Torah observance and his emphasis on preserving the ethnic identities of Jews and non-Jews within the Jesus movement forced him to present Jesus in a way that would form an ideological resource for non-Jewish believers in Jesus—the Gospel of Jesus Christ as Lord.[80]

Conclusion

Paul's discussion of the Torah, and his presentation of Jesus for a non-Jewish audience, was meant to prevent non-Jews from trying to access the God of Israel the way Jews did—through observing the Torah in a covenantal context. This is not to say that Paul believed that the Jewish people should be saved apart from Jesus. But the traditional idea of an absolute conflict between salvation through faith in Jesus and Torah observance is based on an anachronistic Christian understanding of salvation history. In Paul's mind, there was no conflict between observing the Torah and having faith in Jesus *in a Jewish context*.[81] On the contrary, Paul's argument in Rom 9–11 shows that he certainly wanted Jews to accept Jesus as the Messiah of Israel, but it does not suggest that such an acceptance should involve *a repudiation* of the Torah. In fact, from Paul's viewpoint, a contradiction between Jesus as the Messiah and the Torah would seem ridiculous since he probably, as Stowers has put it, "is paralleling and even at points identifying the law with the gospel of God's acts in Jesus Christ."[82]

Of course, Israel will ultimately be saved through God's eschatological instrument—the Messiah. Romans 9–11 clearly shows that Paul expected all Israel to be saved (Rom 11:26) and also that the present "disobedience" of Jewish people was part of God's plan of saving the world. As such, it is even possible to regard the temporary separation of the Jewish people from God as a result of their rejection of Jesus the Messiah as a Christological sacrifice, imitating Jesus' separation from God the Father at the cross.

This soteriological system breaks down when non-Jews claim access to the God of Israel by observing the Torah. According to Paul, the Torah was God's precious gift to the Jewish people and was reserved for Jews. However, through God's messianic instrument, salvation also is now possible for those who did not originally receive the Torah and, in this respect, *and this respect only*, salvation is available apart from Torah observance. In this way, Paul combines a particularistic view of the Torah with a universalistic view of salvation.

Paul's presentation of Jesus as Lord for non-Jewish believers in Jesus was intended to provide them with a role model that would make it possible for them to accept the prevalent situation as well as their ethnic identity. Jesus' suffering under the political power of Rome, his death on the cross, and his humiliation did not change his relation to God. Despite all this, he "became obedient to the point of death" (Phil 2:8). This is the ideal Paul presents his non-Jewish audience with. The reason for this is his firm conviction that every power in heaven and on earth—even death—will finally be conquered. Whatever happens, the true ruler of the world is "*our* Lord Jesus Christ."

4

ELIJAH AND THE MESSIAH AS
SPOKESMEN OF RABBINIC IDEOLOGY[1]

Karin Hedner-Zetterholm

Introduction

The aim of this article is to explore the similarities between
the Messiah and Elijah the Prophet in two important works
of rabbinic literature. The reason for highlighting the
resemblance is twofold: first, Elijah is often associated with
the Messiah, and the two are sometimes presented as performing similar or identical tasks; second, and more impor-
tantly, they seem to be subject to a similar treatment. Due
to the limits of space, this study focuses on two important
rabbinic texts: the Mishnah, which is the earliest rabbinic
document, redacted in the Land of Israel in the early third
century, and the Babylonian Talmud, a rather late compilation, redacted in Babylonia in the fifth to seventh centuries
and probably the most important Jewish text in late antiquity. However, before taking a look at texts from the Mishnah and the Babylonian Talmud, it is helpful to give a brief

and very general survey of the view of the Messiah in rabbinic literature according to recent scholarly opinions.

Messianism in Rabbinic Literature — A Brief Survey

Needless to say, there is no single view of the Messiah in rabbinic literature but rather a great variety of opinions. After all, the group behind this literature, "the rabbis," consisted of many individuals who lived during a period of hundreds of years in two disparate geographical areas, Israel and Babylonia. There are a few general notions that are present in all of rabbinic literature, such as a belief in the coming of the Messiah, the rebuilding of the temple, and the resurrection of the dead; however the disagreements concerning the specific form of these ideas are countless.[2] In spite of this variety, it is possible to discern a distinction between literature from the Tannaitic period (ca 70–250) and that from the Amoraic (ca 250–450) and post-Amoraic periods. The Tannaitic literature contains few messianic references, but the literature from the Amoraic and post-Amoraic periods allow the Messiah a much greater role.

There seems to be a general consensus now that earlier scholarship overemphasized the centrality of messianism to Judaism,[3] partly as a result of reading the sources through the influence of Zionist ideology.[4] Messianism, when it is mentioned in classic rabbinic literature, is essentially a this-worldly political process where the miraculous and supernatural are downplayed. This is particularly true of the Mishnah, which contains very few messianic references. In *Messiah in Context*, J. Neusner argued that the Mishnah is essentially non-messianic and is an expression of a worldview where historical events are considered unimportant. When the Mishnah uses the word Messiah in legal contexts, the meaning is always the anointed priest (*m. Hor.* 2:2–3, 2:7, 3:4), and the Messiah as an apocalyptic figure coming to save Israel at the end of time plays a negligible role. Although there are messianic references, such as "the days of the Messiah" (*m. Ber.* 1:5) and "the footprints of the Messiah" (*m. Soṭah* 9:15), they are the heritage of a messianic past and have no real purpose in the mishnaic presentation of Judaism as a system "aimed at the sanctification of Israel" and with "a teleology lacking an eschatological dimension."[5]

Rabbinic tradition inherited a considerable amount of messianic speculation from the Second Temple period, ideas that were largely preserved in the liturgy, Targums, and folk tradition. Although the rabbinic attitude toward this inheritance was initially negative, the folk tradition proved too strong and by the late Amoraic period, the rabbis were beginning to integrate into their worldview messianic elements in a rabbinic form. This messianism was reshaped so that it served the larger purpose of the Talmud, reinforcing the central idea of rabbinic Judaism, namely the observance of the Torah as it was understood by the rabbis. In direct opposition to the messianic wars of the late first and early second centuries, the rabbis claimed that Israel should not try to hasten the Messiah's arrival through political activities. Instead, God would bring the Messiah when Israel subjects itself to God's rule in observing the Torah. Salvation is made dependent on the behavior of everyday life as expressed in *b. Šabb.* 118b: "If Israel were to keep two Sabbaths according to the laws thereof, they would be redeemed immediately." Thus, the Messiah reenters rabbinic Judaism but in the process is transformed into a tool for the promotion of the worldview of the Babylonian Talmud.[6]

Because we know that messianism played a part in the uprisings against the Romans in 70 and 135 and that popular messianic and prophetic movements existed around the beginning of the common era, as demonstrated by R. Horsley,[7] the reason for the scarcity of messianic references in the Mishnah is usually understood as a wish to suppress messianism rather than reflecting a lack of messianic activities.[8]

According to Horsley, the lack of eschatological expectations in Jewish texts from the beginning of the Common Era does not necessarily mean that such expectations were not common among the ordinary people. He maintains that the fundamental division running through ancient Jewish society was not between Judaism and Hellenism, the Jews and the Romans, or Judaism and Christianity. Rather, it was between the ruled and the rulers, peasants and high priests, and illiterate villagers and the elite literate scribal clients of the aristocracy; and we cannot simply assume that the peasants shared the same views and concerns as the literate elite who authored most of the extant texts from this period. On the contrary, he claims that a careful reading of Josephus suggests widespread messianic activity among the ordinary people. Jewish peasants apparently produced several distinctive movements led by figures recognized as kings. Although they were seen as imposters, false prophets, and charlatans by the aristocratic Pharisee Josephus, who had deserted to the Romans, they appeared as prophets filled with the spirit to the ordinary people. These movements were a revival of the ancient Israelite tradition of popularly elected or "anointed" kings and therefore were appropriately described as messianic movements. During the massive popular uprising following the death of Herod and during the first great revolt against Rome in 66–70, the social-political circumstances provided the occasion for the revival of the popular tradition of kingship for which David provided the principal historical prototype.[9]

In addition to the movements led by figures acclaimed as "kings," there were different kinds of popular prophetic movements during the mid-first century. According to Horsley, the common people were not necessarily dependent on the ruling class of society, such as the Pharisees and

Essenes, but were quite capable of producing their own leaders and movements. Although the messianic movements appear to have been politically involved, often pursuing armed rebellion, the popular prophetic movements seemed mostly to have focused their expectations on superhuman action against the ruling groups. Despite this non-violent character, however, they apparently appeared threatening to the Roman authorities.[10]

The view that the Mishnah's lack of interest in messianism is a reaction against messianic fervor and apocalyptically inspired movements becomes even more compelling when seen in the context of S. Schwartz's claim that many ideas, usually attributed to a separate group often called "apocalyptic Judaism," were profoundly integrated into the main ideology of first-century Judaism. Schwartz argues that the Judaism of the first century was made up of two central ideological axes, of which one was the covenantal ideology centered on God, the temple, and the Torah. The other one was a dualistic mythological narrative that Schwartz calls the apocalyptic myth. According to this apocalyptic myth, one day a struggle between good and evil will come, in which good will win, and God will then rule the world alone, punishing the wicked and rewarding the righteous. According to some versions of the myth, his reign is ushered in by a messianic figure. Although it is common to speak of "apocalyptic Judaism" as a separate movement, Schwartz claims that the apocalyptic myth was incorporated into the main ideology of Judaism with "covenantal Judaism" and the apocalyptic myth forming a single complex. He admits that the myth retained its potential to generate separate social organizations, but there were trends that rejected it altogether, represented by works such as Ben Sira, 1 Maccabees, and possibly Josephus and the Mishnah. Generally, however, he regards these expressions as different trends within a common Judaism that was complex and capacious with blurred boundaries but rejects the idea that different ideologies necessarily represent separate social organizations.[11]

If the apocalyptic ideas were an integrated part of first-century Judaism and not represented only by marginal groups, it may have been even more important for the rabbis of the Mishnah to oppose them in their attempt to establish rabbinic Judaism. The rabbis, who were trying to establish their own authority based on the interpretations of the Torah as opposed to authority based on prophetic inspiration, would naturally want to continue the tradition from Ben Sira and establish a Judaism with few or no traces of the apocalyptic myth.

As Alexander and Neusner have pointed out, in this worldview, which is concerned with defining and achieving piety and dominated by a this-worldly perspective, there is no place for the Messiah.[12] Likewise the Mishnah shows very little interest in historical events and their meaning, possibly as a result of an attempt to build a worldview that ignores the recent terrors.[13] With the Talmud, however, circumstances and rabbinic concerns changed, allowing a greater role for messianism, although in a rabbinic form.

Elijah as the Precursor of the Messiah

The famous prophet Elijah, who according to 2 Kgs 2:11 ascended to heaven without dying, apparently prompted expectations of his eschatological return as attested already within the Hebrew Bible in Mal 3:23–24:

> Lo, I will send the prophet Elijah to you before the coming of the awesome, fearful day of the Lord. He shall reconcile parents with children and children with their parents, so that, when I come, I do not strike the whole land with utter destruction.[14]

Here Elijah is described as returning before the day of judgment to bring about reconciliation[15] and, like the Messiah, is associated with the end of time. Both Elijah and the Messiah are liminal figures who move between heaven and earth, a shared trait that may explain why *Leviticus Rabbah* assigns to them the common task of recording the good deeds of mortals.[16]

A particularly well-known connection between the Messiah and Elijah is Elijah's presence in every Jewish home on the eve of Passover when it is hoped that he will announce the arrival of the Messiah. The festival celebrating the exodus from Egypt was naturally associated with the future redemption and the coming of the Messiah (*b. Roš Haš.* 11a), and through a dispute among the rabbis as to whether the seder ritual required four or five cups of wine, Elijah also became associated with Passover. Since there was an expectation, attested in the Mishnah,[17] that Elijah would resolve doubtful cases of halakhah at his return, the custom arose that the fifth cup should be filled but not drunk (*b. Pesaḥ.* 118a), hence the idea of "Elijah's cup" (*kôsô šel ʾēlîāhû*). This custom may at some point also have been associated with the belief that Elijah would return as the forerunner of the Messiah,[18] an idea that is attested in a few passages in rabbinic literature.[19] For example, in *Pesiqta Rabbati*, dated to a period between the sixth and the ninth centuries, it is stated that "three days before the Messiah comes, Elijah will come and stand upon the mountains of Israel and weep and lament upon them" (35.3).

Until rather recently there was a scholarly consensus that the idea of Elijah as the forerunner of the Messiah was widely known and accepted in the first century. This assumption was considered to explain the identification of John the Baptist, the forerunner of Jesus, with Elijah in the Synoptic Gospels.[20] However, this view has been challenged by other scholars who claim that there is almost no evidence indicating that such a belief was widespread in the first century and that it is more likely that the idea originated with the attempts to interpret the relation between

Jesus and John the Baptist in the New Testament. In their view, the early Jewish belief in Elijah's return concerned only his return before the end of days, as attested in Mal 3:23–24, but this constitutes no proof that he was considered the precursor of the Messiah.[21]

Although pursuing another line of argument, recently C. Milikowsky again defended the concept of Elijah as the forerunner of the Messiah as a pre-Christian idea. In Mal 3:23–24, the return of Elijah is connected to the day of God. Although there is no mention of a messianic figure here, Milikowsky claims that there was a conviction among many Jews that a messianic figure would lead the people on God's day, thus creating a link between the return of Elijah and the coming of the Messiah. In a number of texts from the Second Temple period and from rabbinic literature, the coming of the Messiah is conceived as part of the end of days. However, the majority of rabbinic texts differentiate between the days of the Messiah and the end of days; the days of the Messiah precede the end of days. In this way, when the Messiah was separated from the eschatological future and assigned to his own period ("the days of the Messiah"), the connection between the Messiah and Elijah remained, according to Milikowsky; Elijah then would be seen as a precursor of the Messiah in the same way as he was considered the precursor of the day of God in the Book of Malachi. Milikowsky thinks it unlikely that John the Baptist's role as forerunner to Jesus could generate a notion, entirely unknown until then, that Elijah was to be seen as the precursor to the Messiah and that this idea, which was originally Christian, would have penetrated rabbinic sources.[22] Although it seems a little premature to differentiate so clearly between what was considered Christian and what was considered Jewish as early as the time of the New Testament, Milikowsky has a point in doubting that the interpretation of the relation between Jesus and John the Baptist, completely unknown characters till then, could have created a totally new role for the well-known figure Elijah.

Horsley suggested that although there were certainly expectations of the return of Elijah at the time of Jesus, the more precise idea of Elijah as the forerunner of the Messiah took shape later in a parallel development—that is, among early Christians trying to define the identities and tasks of Jesus and John the Baptist and in rabbinic circles—in an attempt to standardize eschatological doctrines.[23]

The Messiah and Elijah in the Mishnah

As already mentioned, the word "messiah" when used in the Mishnah usually refers to an anointed priest; however, in two passages, the Messiah is spoken of in the context of the end of time and the age to come. Tractate *Berakot* (1:5) speaks of "this world" (*hāʿôlām haze*) as opposed to "the days of the Messiah" (*yĕmôt hamāšîaḥ*), and in tractate *Soṭah* (9:15) there is a reference to "the footprints of the Messiah" (*ʿiqbôt mĕšîḥāʾ*), describing the hardships that will follow the coming of the Messiah. However, as Neusner points out, it is the personal virtues at the very end of the latter passage that are emphasized, and it is those that lead to the resurrection of the dead. The Messiah as a figure coming to save Israel at the end of time has only a minor role.[24] Elijah also is mentioned in this passage (*Soṭah* 9:15) as being responsible for the resurrection of the dead, an event that is usually connected to the messianic age.[25]

> Rabbi Pinhas ben Yair says, diligence [*zĕrîzût*] leads to cleanliness [*nĕqîût*], and cleanliness leads to purity [*ṭāhŏrāh*], and purity leads to abstinence [*pĕrîšût*], and abstinence leads to holiness [*qĕdušāh*], and holiness leads to humility [*ʿănāwāh*], and humility leads to the fear of sin [*yirat ḥēṭʾ*] and fear of sin leads to piety [*ḥăsîdût*], and piety leads to the holy spirit [*rûaḥ*

haqōdeš], and the holy spirit leads to the resurrection of the dead [*teḥîãt hamētîm*], and the resurrection of the dead comes through Elijah, blessed be his memory.

The Mishnah does not reveal anything about the precise relation between the return of Elijah and the coming of the Messiah, but underlying the tasks assigned to Elijah seems to be a tradition, based on Mal 3:23–24, that his return will precede the end of days. As already mentioned, in cases where the rabbis lacked crucial information to settle matters, they were left unresolved "until Elijah will come" (ᶜ*ad šeyãbōʾ ʾēlîãhû*),[26] a phrase that according to *t. Soṭah* 13:2 means "until the dead will live," implying that they would be postponed for an indefinite period of time and possibly solved only with the coming of the Messiah.

I argued elsewhere that the decision to leave a problem for Elijah can be understood as part of the rabbinic struggle against charismatic groups who still believed in the authority of prophets and expected contemporary prophets to solve problems.[27] The Second Temple period seems to have been a sort of middle ground, where some Jews believed that prophecy had ceased, but others continued to believe in prophetic activity. Josephus obviously believed in prophets and prophecy in his time, even though he perceived some sort of distinction between the ancient prophets and prophetic figures of his day.[28] In the New Testament, the existence of prophets seems to be widely assumed (Matt 14:5; Mark 11:32; Luke 24:19; John 4:19). The rabbis insist in numerous places that prophecy had ceased in their time,[29] but it is possible that, originally, this insistence was not so much a statement of fact but part of a struggle against groups who still believed in prophets.

It is a well-known fact that the early rabbinic movement transformed biblical figures as well as contemporary charismatic figures in an attempt to establish for themselves the religious authority that previously belonged to others. Previous scholarship on Palestinian charismatic figures of the first century, such as Jesus, Honi the Circle-Drawer, and Hanina ben Dosa, has shown that rabbinic sources indicate a tension between charismatic figures and rabbis in the first century. According to most scholars, this tension was predicated primarily upon the issue of authority. Individuals claiming access to God outside of the rabbinic structure, charismatic figures who claimed supernatural powers, miracle-workers, or prophets would have presented a challenge to the rabbis' claims to authority.[30] To defer a problem to Elijah would be "safe," so to speak, as he was expected only at the end of days and, accordingly, posed no threat to rabbinic authority.

Common to the Messiah and Elijah, as presented in the Mishnah, is a general lack of interest and a relatively insignificant role assigned to them. They both seem to be victims of the rabbis' wish to suppress apocalyptic and revolutionary tendencies in an attempt to establish rabbinic Judaism.

The Messiah and Elijah in the Babylonian Talmud

The most extensive discussion of the Messiah in the Babylonian Talmud appears in *Sanh.* 96b–99a, where Elijah also appears in two episodes. Despite the fact that much of the material in this *sugya* is presented as *baraitot*, most of it probably dates to the Amoraic period and may have been redacted even later.[31] A few main points emerge from this passage:

1. The coming of the Messiah will be preceded by a time of trouble. Grief and evil will abound, there will be famine, pious men will die, scholars will be few, and the Torah will be forgotten. The young will insult the old, impudence will increase, and God-fearing men will be despised.

2. One should not try to calculate the time of the coming of the Messiah, because erroneous calculations may lead some people to believe that he will never come.

3. It is the condition of Israel that determines when the Messiah will come. Israel will repent either because of their righteousness or because God will make them repent against their will.

4. The Messiah will come from the house of David and is most often referred to as "the son of David."[32]

There is a strong emphasis on Israel's sins and on the power of repentance, both to overcome sin and bring the Messiah. However, the opposite opinion is also recorded, namely that Israel will be redeemed even without repentance (*b. Sanh.* 97b):

> Rav said, "All of the dates that have been designated [for the arrival of the Messiah] have passed, and the matter [now] depends only on repentance and good deeds." But Shmuel [disagreed] and said, "It is sufficient for a mourner to keep his [period] of mourning."

The continuation of the passage relates a discussion between Rabbi Eliezer and Rabbi Yehoshua. The former holds the opinion that repentance is a necessary prerequisite for redemption, whereas the latter believes that Israel will be redeemed through God's initiative alone at a predetermined time even without repentance.[33] This passage attests to two opposing views on redemption. One, represented by Rabbi Yehoshua, is an eschatology focused upon miraculous intervention by God at a predetermined time irrespective of Israel's condition, and the other, represented by Rabbi Eliezer, emphasizes repentance as the way to bring about salvation.

It has been suggested that the view that Israel would be

"He is sitting among the poor lepers. They all untie and retie [their bandages] at one time but he unties and reties [each bandage] separately saying [to himself], 'Perhaps I will be wanted, I should not delay.'" He [Rabbi Yehoshua ben Levi] came to him and said to him, "Peace be with you rabbi my master and teacher." He replied, "Peace be with you, son of Levi." He [Rabbi Yehoshua ben Levi] said to him, "When will you come, Master?" He said to him, "Today." He [Rabbi Yehoshua ben Levi] went back to Elijah and he [Elijah] asked him, "What did he tell you?" "Peace be with you, son of Levi," he answered. Elijah said, "[With those words] he promised you and your father entrance into the world to come." [But] he [Rabbi Yehoshua ben Levi] said, "He lied to me because he said that he would come today and he has not come!" He [Elijah] said, "This is what he meant, *Today if you will listen to his voice*" [Ps 95:7].

This story is introduced with the phrase "Rabbi So-and-So met Elijah" [*rabbi pĕlônî ʾaškaḥ lĕʾēlîāhû*], an expression that is found only in the Babylonian Talmud and in midrashim that postdate it, indicating that it is part of a rather late reworking.[39] The main source of this story seems to be a passage in the Jerusalem Talmud (*y. Taʿan.* 1:1), rendered here in an abbreviated form:[40]

Rabbi Yehoshua ben Levi said, "If someone should say to you, 'Where is your God?' Tell him, 'In the great city that is in Rome.'" What is the reason? [the scriptural basis?] *My God calls from Seir* [Isa 21:11].[41] Rabbi Shimon ben Yohai taught, "In every place where Israel was exiled, the Shekhinah was exiled with them . . . . They were exiled to Rome and the Shekhinah was exiled with them. What is the reason? *My God calls from Seir, Watchman, what of the*

night?" [Isa 21:11]. Israel said to Isaiah, "Isaiah, our rabbi, what will this night bring us?" He said to them, "Wait for me until the question is asked." When he had asked the question he returned to them . . . He said to them, "It is not what you are thinking but there will be morning for the righteous, and night for the wicked, morning for Israel, and night for the nations of the world." They said to him, "When?" He said to them, "Whenever you want, he too wants it. *If you want it, ask"* [Isa 21:12]. They said to him, "What is preventing it?" He said to them, "Repentance, *Come back again"* [Isa 21:12]. Rabbi Aha said in the name of Rabbi Tanhum ben Rabbi Hiyya, "If Israel repents for one day, the son of David would come immediately." What is the reason? *Today, if you will listen to his voice* [Ps 97:5]. Rabbi Levi said, "If Israel would keep a single Sabbath in the proper way, the son of David would come immediately."

Using a technique common to the storytellers of the Babylonian Talmud, the story in the Jerusalem Talmud has been reworked and embellished, taking the mention of Rabbi Yehoshua ben Levi as a starting point for developing a whole episode involving him and Elijah.[42] Instead of the passage in the Jerusalem Talmud where Rabbi Yehoshua ben Levi explains that God has gone into exile to Rome with his people, the Babylonian Talmud has a direct conversation between Rabbi Yehoshua ben Levi and the Messiah who is suffering among the poor and sick at the gates of the wicked city of Rome, eagerly awaiting a sign from Israel that it is time for him to deliver them.[43] It is also significant that whereas the Jerusalem Talmud presents the prophet Isaiah as the mediator between Israel and God, the Babylonian Talmud has Elijah, an indication of the special use that the Babylonian Talmud makes of him.

The point of the story is apparently to emphasize the idea

that the coming of the Messiah is dependent on Israel's behavior, as explained by Elijah at the end: "Today, if you will listen to his voice." While this message is present in the story from the Jerusalem Talmud as well, the Babylonian reworking strongly emphasizes it by adding the story involving Elijah and the Messiah. The Messiah's prompt answer that he will come today comes as a surprise, since the audience knows that he himself does not know when he will come to redeem Israel, creating a contradiction that again draws attention to the point of the story. "Today" is not a fixed date but means that the Messiah will come when the Jewish people listen to God's voice.

Questions about the arrival of the Messiah occur a number of times in *b. Sanh.* 96b–99a.[44] It is striking that, while the rabbis all come up with some kind of answer, the Messiah himself does not know, and Elijah, whose role is to always answer the questions posed to him, refrains from answering. If the Messiah himself does not know when he is coming and if Elijah, who possesses divine knowledge and knows where to find the Messiah and explain his answer, does not know either, then nobody, not even God, knows. God, the Messiah, and Elijah are all powerless; only the Jewish people are capable of bringing the Messiah through repentance and proper behavior. The fact that it is the Messiah who quotes the scriptural verse, "Today," and it is Elijah—rather than merely a rabbi as in the story in the Jerusalem Talmud—who explains that it means that the Messiah will come today if only you listen to his voice, elevates this statement from being an opinion among others to being the truth. This way of using Elijah to voice the opinion of the storytellers seems to be characteristic of the Babylonian Talmud.[45]

Another passage involving both Elijah and the Messiah is the story in *b. B. Meṣiʿa* 85b where some rabbis, with the help of information revealed by Elijah, try to bring the Messiah before the appointed time:

Elijah would frequently visit Rabbi's (Rabbi Yehudah ha-Nasi) academy. One day of the New Moon he was delayed and did not come [at the usual hour]. He [Rabbi Yehudah] asked him, "Why were you delayed, sir?" He [Elijah] said, "[I waited until] I had awakened Abraham and washed his hands. Then he prayed and I laid him down to sleep and then [I did the same] with Isaac and Jacob. [Rabbi Yehudah said], "And [why not] wake them up together?" [Elijah said], "I thought they might be so strong in prayer that they would bring the Messiah before the appointed time" [lit. not in his time]. He [Rabbi Yehudah] said, "Are there others like them in this world?" He [Elijah] said, "There are Rabbi Hiyya and his sons." Rabbi proclaimed a fast and had Rabbi Hiyya and his sons go down [to the ark]. He [Rabbi Hiyya] said, "He causes the wind to blow," and a strong wind blew. He said, "He causes the rain to fall," and rain came. When he was about to say, "He resurrects the dead," the world shook. They said in heaven, "Who has revealed the secret on earth?" They said, "Elijah." They brought in Elijah and struck him with sixty lashes of fire. He came and appeared as a fiery bear among them and drove them away.

This passage appears immediately after a story about a rabbi whose eyes were burned from looking at Rabbi Hiyya's chariot despite a warning from Elijah, and it concludes a group of stories that praise the power of Rabbi Hiyya. Like the preceding one, this story seems to warn against human involvement with things that belong to the heavenly realm and advocates appropriate exercise of human power.[46] In both these stories, Elijah, upon request, reveals potentially dangerous heavenly knowledge, and in our story he is punished for it with sixty lashes of fire, a punishment that recalls the fate of the rabbi in the previous story who was struck in the eyes with fire, as well as the punishment of two supernatural beings, Metatron and Gabriel, who were also struck with sixty lashes of fire (*maḥyûhû šitîn pûlsēy dĕnûrāʾ*) according to two other passages in the Babylonian Talmud. In *b. Hag.* 15a, the angel Metatron receives sixty lashes of fire for leading Elisha ben Abuya to mistakenly conclude that there is another divinity in heaven besides God; in *b. Yoma* 77a, the archangel Gabriel gets the same punishment for acting independently of God's will. According to *b. B. Meṣiʿa* 47a, this is a particularly severe form of punishment and may even imply excommunication.[47]

In our story, Elijah is also punished for acting independently of God's will by revealing the secret of human power. By not taking the risk of having the three patriarchs pray together and thereby bringing the Messiah before the appointed time, Elijah shows that he knows that one should not try to hasten the arrival of the Messiah. Nevertheless, he reveals the secret of how to do it to Rabbi Yehudah ha-Nasi, letting him decide whether to make use of that knowledge or not. Supporting human freedom is a characteristic of Elijah,[48] but this time he apparently goes too far and is the one to be punished rather than the rabbi trying to make use of his information. In all three cases involving sixty lashes of fire, the punishment is not carried out by God but by an anonymous "they," and they all lack a statement of God's disapproval, perhaps implying that God approves of the goals of these rabbis but not their means.[49]

The rabbis themselves appear ambivalent concerning the possibility to hasten the arrival of the Messiah. To be sure, they longed for the messianic era, but at the same time, they seem to experience a certain relief when hastening it proves impossible. If God has set a time for the coming of the Messiah and his arrival cannot be hastened or forced, the rabbis' authority remains solid.[50] Or, perhaps the suggestion that a certain person, even if he is a rabbi, has the power to change the world order by means of powerful prayer, was unsettling.[51] It certainly is not consistent with the idea expressed elsewhere that if only Israel repents and is faithful to the Torah, the Messiah will come. Possibly Elijah reflects this ambivalence by first taking part in the attempt to bring the Messiah before his time and then preventing it at the last moment. In any case, common to this story and those at *b. Sanh.* 98a is the idea that hastening or predicting the coming of the Messiah is impossible, thus serving to uphold rabbinic authority.

Conclusions

The idea that it is the condition of the Jewish people that determines the coming of the Messiah seems to be the most favored one in the Babylonian Talmud, although traces of other notions remain. This idea helps explain why the Messiah has not come despite scriptural predictions,[52] as well as being a powerful message of hope, giving a sense of mastery of one's destiny.[53] From the point of view of the rabbis, it also had several advantages. Making the arrival of the Messiah dependant on Israel's observance of the Torah, according to the rabbinic understanding, greatly strengthened the rabbinic system, serving to preserve things pretty much as they were, while at the same time promising dramatic change. Being antithetical to the idea of actively bringing the Messiah, it discouraged political rebellion and favored an attitude of accepting hardship and waiting.[54] If the coming of the Messiah cannot be forced or accurately predicted, the rabbis' authority remains solid.[55] This strengthening of the rabbinic system by making the coming of the Messiah dependant on observance of the Torah, then, would be an expression of what D. Boyarin has recently called the "rabbinic take-over of religious life and practice."[56]

While the rabbis of the Mishnah, as a reaction against the apocalyptic and messianic wars of the late first and early second centuries, downplayed the significance of the Messiah as an apocalyptic figure coming to save Israel at the end of time, the rabbis of the two Talmuds reintroduced formerly neglected ideas of the Messiah, transforming them in the process. In Neusner's words: "So while the Talmuds introduced a formerly neglected myth, their version of the Messiah became precisely what the sages of the Mishnah and their continuators in the Talmud most needed: a rabbi-Messiah, who would save an Israel sanctified through Torah. Salvation then depends upon sanctification, and is subordinated to it."[57]

It is interesting to note that Elijah is subject to a similar treatment in rabbinic literature and, in all likelihood, his transformation from prophet to rabbi, eventually depriving him of all eschatological traits, also has to do with the issue of rabbinic authority. Just as the Messiah, viewed as an eschatological figure, could be a perceived as a threat to rabbinic authority, prophets with insight into the divine will could likewise undermine the rabbinic program of establishing their legitimacy and power through the interpretation of the Torah. Moreover, Elijah and the Messiah were both originally connected to the end of time, a period when the validity of rabbinic authority might not be obvious.

It is true that biblical figures in general are transformed in rabbinic literature and are presented as observing the Torah according to the rabbinic interpretation of it, probably as a way of legitimizing rabbinic tradition by implying in this way that the rabbis' understanding of Judaism already was revealed at Sinai. However, the transformation of Elijah in particular seems to reflect the rabbinic struggle for authority and legitimacy. By refashioning the biblical Elijah, a prophet with charismatic and eschatological traits, to Elijah the rabbi, who discusses points of halakhah and aggadah with other rabbis, the rabbis simultaneously reject

the claims of contemporary prophets and charismatic figures and bolster their own claim to be the ones who medi-
ate God's word to Israel.

I have argued elsewhere that the rabbis dealt with the
remains of Elijah's prophetic powers in two different ways.
On the one hand, they were careful to keep Elijah out of the
area of halakhah by limiting his prophetic knowledge to
factual information, subordinating his opinion to rabbinic
authority, and by insisting that halakhic problems not be
deferred to Elijah since they themselves have the authority
to solve the issue without access to factual information or
divine truth. On the other hand, they put Elijah's prophetic
knowledge in their service. In a number of stories in the
Babylonian Talmud, Elijah as God's messenger affirms the
rabbinic right to legislate and interpret the Torah, and in
this function, his insight into God's will becomes a resource
serving the interest of the rabbis. [58]

Deprived of their eschatological traits and incorporated
into the rabbinic system, both Elijah and the Messiah prove
useful in promoting the rabbinic worldview; the Messiah
by making his own arrival dependant on observance of the
Torah, and Elijah by providing divine affirmation of rabbinic ideology.[59] This is particularly evident in the Babylonian Talmud where the similarities between Elijah and
the Messiah go beyond shared traits and responsibilities,
both being important figures in promoting the ideology of
this Talmud.

5

THE RECEPTION OF MESSIANISM AND THE WORSHIP OF CHRIST IN THE POST-APOSTOLIC CHURCH

Jan-Eric Steppa

The Legitimacy of the Christian Messiah

Opposition and Legitimacy

From the days of the earliest Christian expansion into the Gentile world, a very long time would elapse before Christians were taken seriously by polytheistic intellectuals. The first critics of the Christian movement, Pliny the Younger, Tacitus, and Suetonius,[1] spoke of Christianity as being a debased or mischievous superstition, a foreign cult regarded as a potential threat to the traditional Roman way of life and religious customs. These early critics of Christianity, however, had little or no interest in the Christian religion. Even Pliny, the governor of Bithynia-Pontus in northwestern Asia Minor, in 112 CE performed only a halfhearted investigation of local Christians' beliefs and practices after receiving complaints from a group of pagan citizens. In fact, knowledge of the Christian religion, its writings and liturgical practices, and its relationship to the Jewish tradition was vague at best. Like Pliny, many outside observers of early Christianity probably knew that Christians gathered before daybreak on a certain day of the week for secret worship. However, they did not know much of what was going on at those secret assemblies, though some observers may have associated the activities of the Christians with the obscure rites in religious associations such as the Bacchic mysteries. Blurry perceptions of the Christian celebration of the Eucharist seem to have stirred the fantasies of the contemporaries; causing the spread of rumors about clandestine nocturnal ceremonies with feasting and drinking and involving promiscuity, incest, infanticide, cannibalism, and a variety of other bizarre rites.[2] Such allegations, together with charges of "atheism," implying disloyalty and insolence toward the ancient religious traditions of the Romans, helped to fortify popular hostility to Christians, which prompted sporadic pogroms and persecutions.

The apparent indifference in early anti-Christian literature to what Christians actually believed can be considered as one aspect of the popular construction of the Christian "other" as a dangerous threat to the social and religious stability of the Roman society. Particularly in the period between 150 and 180 CE, when Christians were frequently subject to mob violence and persecutions by local governors often under pressure from the anti-Christian crowds, popular hatred against Christians seems to have been based almost solely on rumors.[3]

It was during these times of anti-Christian propaganda and persecution that Christians for the first time were confronted by pagan opponents who articulated their polemics with a much more serious and sophisticated approach. In the latter part of the second century CE, the illustrious physician and philosopher Galen included in his pharmacological writings critical comments against both Christians and Jews. He criticized the observers of both religions for being dogmatic and irrational and expressed his dissatisfaction with their tendency to blend reason with revelation and science with faith. Nevertheless, he considered both Christianity and Judaism not as foreign superstitions but as philosophical schools, and although he deemed Christianity a deficient philosophy, he appreciated Christians for pursuing a disciplined and virtuous life.[4] Thus, the first step was taken for Christianity to be acknowledged as a legitimate religion in the Greco-Roman world. But toward the end of the second century, the legitimacy of the Christian religion still was contested by intellectual Romans, profoundly suspicious of new beliefs that were not founded on ancient ancestral traditions. A traditionalistic attitude most clearly expressed in the early third century by Dio Cassius in his *Roman History* (52.36), reporting on Maecenas's speech before the emperor Augustus, was that true religion should be kept unsoiled by innovations and foreign practices:

> Those who attempt to distort our religion with strange rites you should abhor and punish, not merely for the sake of the gods (since if a man despises these he will not pay honour to any other being), but because such men, by bringing in new divinities in place of the old, persuade many to adopt foreign practices, from which spring up conspiracies, factions, and cabals, which are far from profitable to a monarchy. Do not, therefore, permit anybody to be an atheist or a sorcerer.[5]

From this perspective, Christianity was not only a foreign, non-Roman religion with suspicious social, cultural, and political implications. It also was an awkwardly recent religious movement that had emerged in Palestine during the reign of Emperor Tiberius and thus impossible for conservative Romans to take seriously.[6]

Pagan attacks against the legitimacy of Christianity based on arguments about Christians' lack of history and ancestral foundation did not pass unnoticed among intellectual Christians. In the most well-known and perhaps also the most interesting of his thirty-one extant works, the *Apology*, composed about 198 CE, the North African theologian Tertullian presents a forceful response to the critique of Christianity as a religion without tradition and history and consequently, without any convincing claim to truth. In fact, Tertullian's *Apology* is all about history, using historical arguments not only to strengthen the legitimacy of Christianity, but also to discredit the historical claim of Roman traditions. In the text, Tertullian makes a fierce attack against the Roman belief in the unchangeable nature of their ancestral traditions. In *Apol.* 6.9–10, Tertullian argues that instead of promoting stability, the ancient traditions are subverted by decadence and decay:

> What has come to your religion—of the veneration due by you to your ancestors? In your dress, in your food, in your style of life, in your opinions, and last of all in your very speech, you have renounced your progenitors. You are always praising antiquity, and yet every day you have novelties in your way of living.[7]

Later on in the *Apology*, Tertullian challenges the very idea of the antiquity of the Roman gods and questions the prevalent notion of a necessary relationship between the greatness and prosperity of the Romans and the favor of their gods (*Apol.* 26.2):

> Rome of rural simplicity is older than some of her gods; she reigned before her proud, vast Capitol was built. The Babylonians exercised dominion, too,

before the days of the Pontiffs; and the Medes before the Quindecemvirs; and the Egyptians before the Salii; and the Assyrians before the Luperci; and the Amazons before the Vestal Virgins.

In his historiographical deconstruction of Roman traditions as foundation for attacks on Christians, Tertullian turns to the Jewish religion to further his relativization of the Roman claim for national and religious antiquity. Against the background of the close relationship between authority and antiquity, he presents the Jewish Scriptures as being the oldest writings in the world, containing all the treasures of the Jewish religion and, consequently, also those of the Christian religion.[8] Through Moses he then specifies the age of these writings, demonstrating their origin to be far more ancient than the oldest Roman records (*Apol.* 19.3–4).

If you happen to have heard of a certain Moses . . . he is as far back as the Argive Inachus; by nearly four hundred years—only seven less—he precedes Danaus, your most ancient name; while he antedates by a millennium the death of Priam. I might affirm, too, that he is five hundred years earlier than Homer, and have supporters of that view. The other prophets also, though of later date, are, even the most recent of them, as far back as the first of your philosophers, and legislators, and historians.

For Tertullian, the Jewish Scriptures were not only to be considered the most ancient of all writings, but they were also loaded with divine inspiration. Proof for the divinity of the Scriptures could be found in the abundance of prophetic messages about real historic events, such as the destruction of cities by earthquakes, the sinking of islands, wars, collisions of kingdoms with other kingdoms, famines, pestilence, massacres, decay of righteousness, and the growth of sin, and so forth.[9]

Though Tertullian emphasizes that Christians claim the Jewish Scriptures as their own and defends the legitimacy of the Christian religion through the antiquity and divine inspiration of these Scriptures, he is forced to admit that Christianity may appear as a relatively young religious movement, dating its emergence not earlier than the reign of Emperor Tiberius. Everyone also could see that the Christians, in spite of their confident claim of sharing their history and traditions with the Jews, were certainly not in line with the Jews when it came to observance of Jewish food regulations, celebration of Jewish festivals, and the practice of circumcision. Tertullian is well aware of that objection but attaches no great importance to these differences in religious practices when dealing with the essential difference between the Christians and the Jews. Instead the real point of divergence between Christians and Jews, in Tertullian's view, concerned the coming of the Messiah (*Apol.* 21.15).

> The Jews, too, were well aware that Christ was coming, as those to whom the prophets spake. Nay, even now His advent is expected by them; nor is there any other contention between them and us; than that they believe the advent has not yet occured.

Tertullian thus reduces the difference between Christianity and Judaism to a matter of believing or not believing that Jesus Christ was the Messiah whose coming had been foretold in the prophecies of the Scriptures. Having proven themselves more faithful through their acceptance of Jesus as the Coming One, Christians had merited God's favor. The Jews, in turn, had been deprived of that favor as a result of their rejection of Christ.[10] In Tertullian's anti-Jewish polemic, the Jews had grown blind to their own Scriptures and its promises of the coming of the Messiah. Those who previously flourished under God were therefore no longer

God's people but were condemned to suffer, "[s]cattered abroad, a race of wanderers, exiles from their own land and clime, they roam over the whole world without either a human or a heavenly king."[11] This is taken as an evident testimony for their impiety.

The Old Testament prophecies about the coming Messiah were thus adopted by the Christians, whereas prophecies of doom were perceived by Christians as confirmed by the fall of the Jewish nation, attributing these contemporary events to divine punishment for their rejection of Jesus as the foretold Messiah.[12] Thus, the Christian acceptance of Jesus as the Messiah and the Jewish rejection of this idea stand as the great dividing line between the two religions.

Justin Martyr's Messiah

A particularly explicit account of the division between Christianity and Judaism is found in Justin Martyr's *Dialogue with Trypho*, composed in Rome about 160 CE in the form of a fictitious debate in Ephesus between the author and a learned Jew named Trypho. In the dialogue, Trypho blames the Christians for forsaking God and the observances of the law by placing their trust in a mere man. Justin puts the following ironic words into Trypho's mouth (*Dial.* 8.4):

> Christ—if He has indeed been born, and exists anywhere—is unknown, and does not even know Himself, and has no power until Elias come to anoint Him, and make Him manifest to all. And you, having accepted a groundless report, invent a Christ for yourselves, and for his sake are inconsiderately perishing.[13]

It is not unlikely that these words correspond to contemporary Jewish sentiments concerning Christian messianism.

Neither are there any reasons to doubt that the dialogue reflects actual debates in the middle of the second century between intellectual, Hellenic-minded Jews and Christians.[14]

Apart from the authenticity of the scene rendered by Justin, it is evident that one dominating concern in the dialogue is to defend the Christian claim of Jesus as the Messiah of the Scriptures. To Trypho's objection against the Christian application of the messianic prophecies to Jesus, Justin replies immediately that such a failure to recognize Jesus as the Messiah arises from a lack of understanding of the true meaning of the Scriptures.[15] When Trypho objects to the idea that the Messiah was subjected to shameful crucifixion and death[16] and questions the Christians' blasphemous claim of divine status to such a Messiah,[17] Justin responds confidently with Christian interpretations of the messianic proof texts from the Old Testament. However, when defending his Christological messianism against the objections of Trypho, he employs not only the prophecies about the Coming One, but also uses Old Testament theophanies to demonstrate Christ as the preexistent Logos. Thus it was Christ as the Son-Logos who in Gen 18 visited Abraham under the oak in Mamre and spoke to him,[18] and it was the Son-Logos whom God referred to when speaking to Moses about Joshua in Exod 23:20–21.[19] As proof texts, Justin also considers the places in the Old Testament where "Lord" and "God" occur, referring to someone other than God the Creator of all things. For instance, in his conversation with Trypho, Justin provides messianic interpretations to Ps 110:1 ("The Lord says to my Lord")[20] and Ps 45:7–8 ("Therefore God, your God, has anointed you with the oil of gladness beyond your companions").[21] To legitimize this interpretative strategy, Justin explicitly declares that "it must be admitted absolutely that some other one is called Lord by the Holy Spirit besides Him who is considered Maker of all things" (*Dial.* 56.14).

Justin's treatment of the Old Testament as source for

proof texts for the authenticity of Jesus as the awaited Messiah reflects a "binitarian" tradition of worship that is represented most clearly in the New Testament by Heb 1, with its list of proof texts adopted for the justification of a "two-ishness" of the monotheistic commitment. In fact, for the later development of trinitarian theology in the early church, the tradition of selecting and employing messianic proof texts had considerable importance for the later development of trinitarian theology in the early church. In this process of defining the duality on the basis of messianic interpretation of the Old Testament, Justin played a key role together with Irenaeus and Tertullian, also belonging to the proof-text tradition of the post-apostolic age.[22]

The importance of Old Testament proof texts for the legitimacy of Christian messianism in the earliest Christian literature also had a crucial effect on the relationship between Christian and Jewish understanding and interpretation of the Scriptures. The Christian claims of Jesus as the Coming One not only caused a constant battle between alternative readings of scriptural passages, but also a conflict over the possession of the Scriptures. Justin, stating his opinion that circumcision is useless for those who have Christ, does not mince his words about his view on Jewish interpretation of the Scriptures (*Dial.* 29.1):

What need, then, have I of circumcision, who have been witnessed to by God? What need have I of that other baptism, who have been baptized with the Holy Ghost? I think that while I mention this, I would persuade even those who are possessed of scanty intelligence. For these words have neither been prepared by me, nor embellished by the art of man; but David sung them, Isaiah preached them, Zechariah proclaimed them, and Moses wrote them. Are you acquainted with them, Trypho? They are contained in your Scriptures, or rather not yours, but

ours. For we believe them; but you, though you read
them, do not catch the spirit that is in them.

For Justin, the failure of the Jews to comprehend the numerous scriptural evidences for the messiahship of Jesus completely disqualified them from possession of the Scriptures.
Justin expresses here an uncompromising view of the trans-
ference of God's favor from the Jews to the Christians. From
the moment of the Jews' rejection of Christ as the Messiah,
Christians have become the rightful descendants of Judah,
Jacob, Isaac, and Abraham, and thus the true spiritual
Israel.[23] Toward the end of the dialogue (*Dial.* 136.3), Justin
delivers an even more explicit judgment against the Jews,
accusing them not only of blasphemous ungratefulness
toward the promises of God but also of hatred against those
who believe in Christ:

> [Y]ou have not accepted God's Christ. For he who
> knows not Him, knows not the will of God; and he
> who insults and hates Him, insults and hates Him
> that sent Him. And whoever believes not in Him,
> believes not the declarations of the prophets, who
> preached and proclaimed Him to all.

The harshness of Justin's tone in his attacks on Judaism,
marking the beginning of a long history of demonization of
the Jews, hardly corresponds to the surprisingly gentle and
calm attitude of Trypho throughout most of the debate.
Nevertheless, in the eyes of Justin, the Jews not only reject
Christ as the foretold Messiah but also are filled with hate
and hostility toward both Christ and Christians. They curse
and condemn Christians and Christ himself, and Justin
even accuses Jews of murdering Christians.[24] Even though
he does not mention Christian aggression against Jews,
Justin's charges of Jewish harassment and persecution of
Christians may well give accurate and trustworthy information of deep mutual hostility prevailing between Chris-

tianity and Judaism in the ante-Constantinian era. A number of treatises directed exclusively against Jews were composed in the post-apostolic age by prominent Christian authors, such as Tertullian, Cyprian, and Hippolytus. The *Adversus Iudaeus* literature of the early church corresponded to anti-Christian polemic in the Jewish rabbinic sources. Contemporary Jewish critique against Christian messianic claims may also be present in at least one non-Jewish text, *On the True Doctrine*, composed by the Platonist philosopher Celsus about 178 CE.

Celsus and Origen

Celsus's *On the True Doctrine* marks the very first serious literary attack on Christianity and reflects the opinions of a particularly well-informed and well-read intellectual, observing the Christians and their practices and ideas from a strict traditionalistic Greco-Roman viewpoint. The text itself is preserved only in fragments from which it is possible to reconstruct at least the main arguments of the work. What still remains of *On the True Doctrine* is contained in what is to be recognized as one of the most important apologetic works of early Christianity, namely Origen's *Contra Celsum*, written about seventy years after the composition of *On the True Doctrine*. From Origen's extensive quotes from *On the True Doctrine*, it is evident that Celsus possessed detailed knowledge about Christianity that enabled him to find the most vulnerable points of the Christian religion and subject them to satirical irony. Many times his critique was aimed at concrete expressions of Christian faith and often founded on his own philosophical positions. There can be no doubt that Celsus was deeply acquainted with Christian literature, not only with the Scriptures but also Christian apologetic texts. It even has been suggested that *On the True Doctrine* was composed as a reply to Justin Martyr's apologetic writings.[25] In the beginning of the second book of *Contra Celsum* (2.1), the objections of Trypho against the Christians is echoed in Celsus's accusation of Christian converts from Judaism, put into the mouth of a Jewish spokesman:

> What induced you, my fellow-citizens, to abandon the law of your fathers, and to allow your minds to be led captive by him with whom we have just conversed, and thus be most ridiculously deluded, so as to become deserters from us to another name, and to the practices of another life?[26]

And later in the text, Celsus continues by letting his Jewish spokesman address himself directly to the Christians: "How is it that you take the beginning of your system from our worship, and when you have made some progress you treat it with disrespect, although you have no other foundation to show for your doctrines than our law?" (*Cels.* 2.4).

Thus, the Christian claim that it rests firmly on the heritage of the Jewish religion appears as one of the main points of departure for Celsus's criticism of Christianity. Celsus was certainly well aware of the strength of this attack. He knew that the Christian claim to truth was dependent on ancient Jewish traditions and that the Christians based their religion on a self-confident, but in his view a fundamentally false, assertion of being the rightful inheritors of those traditions. The Christians claimed to be true children of the Jewish law, yet they did not in any respect observe the Law. In *Cels.* 7.18 Celsus asks:

> Whether is it Moses or Jesus who teaches falsely? Did the Father, when he sent Jesus, forget the commands which he had given to Moses? Or did he change his mind, condemn his own laws, and send forth a messenger with counter instructions?

Anti-Christian polemicists before Celsus paid very little attention to the figure of Jesus and dealt exclusively with alleged shortcomings of Christians. Celsus was the first anti-Christian writer who directed his critique immediately against the Christian exaltation of Jesus. In Celsus's eyes, Jesus was nothing but a magician, one of many self-claimed sorcerers who could be found everywhere in the Roman Empire and "who in the middle of the marketplace, in return for a few obols, will impart the knowledge of their most venerated arts, and will expel demons from men, and dispel diseases, and invoke the souls of heroes" (*Cels.* 1.68).

In his attempt to completely demolish the Christian worship of Jesus as the son of God, Celsus deconstructed the mythologies that surrounded the figure of Jesus by providing an alternative account of his life. Jesus' mother became "a poor woman of the country, who subsisted by spinning and who was turned out of doors by her husband, a carpenter by trade, because she was convicted of adultery" (*Cels.* 1.28), and "she bore a child to a certain soldier named Panthera" (*Cels.* 1.32). Celsus further observes that the messianic claim associated by the Christians to Jesus was far from being acknowledged by the Jews in spite of the fact that they long had expected him. For Celsus, Jesus was not just a mere man. He was a deceiver as well, leading his followers astray when they were progressing in the Jewish observance of the law.[27]

In his *On the True Doctrine*, Celsus thus delivered a serious attack on Christian messianism. Christianity, for Celsus, was nothing but an apostasy from Judaism, and the Christian claim that Jesus was the foretold Messiah was unjustified.[28] The Jew who appears as Celsus's spokesman objects to Christian messianism by explaining that "the prophets declare the coming one to be a mighty potentate, Lord of all nations and armies" (*Cels.* 2.29). He points out that Jesus certainly was no "good general," since he lacked the ability to inspire his followers to "that feeling of goodwill which so to speak, would be manifested towards a brigand chief" (*Cels.* 2.12). Origen, in turn, replies that Jesus indeed was to be considered as a potentate, for "righteousness has arisen in his days, and there is abundance of peace, which took its commencement at his birth, God preparing the nations for His teaching, that they might be under one prince, the king of the Romans" (*Cels.* 2.30).

In this way, Origen establishes an intimate connection between the messianic kingship of Christ on the one hand, and, on the other hand, the universal authority of the Roman emperor and the blessed state of *Pax Romana* that not only facilitated the spreading of the Christian faith throughout the empire through the command "Go therefore and make disciples of all nations" (Matt 28:19), but that also corresponded to the gospel's teaching of peace, which according to Origen, "does not permit men to take vengeance even upon enemies" (*Cels.* 2.30). The peace and greatness of the Roman Empire, thus, is a reflection of the messianic power and glory of Christ.

However, Origen does not provide a full reply to the main problem for Celsus, as well as for his Jewish contemporaries concerning Christian messianism. This is the seemingly non-messianic character of Jesus' earthly career from the point of view of the Jewish hope for the emergence of a king-Messiah. In fact, there is little talk about the messianic kingship of Christ in the *Contra Celsum*. This can be explained against the background of the lack of interest within the Hellenistic Judaism of Alexandria for the eschatological messianism, which was prevalent in Palestinian Judaism. The Hellenistic allegorical tradition, which began with Philo and developed into the Christian tradition by Clement of Alexandria and Origen, seems to have forced into the background the typological interpretation of Scripture, which may have formed the exegetical basis for a Christian messianism. The legacy of Palestinian Jewish messianism, evident in Hebrews, *Barnabas*, and Justin Martyr's *Dialogue with Trypho*, where Christ appears as the eschatological King, seems absent in Alexandrian theology. Surely we find Christ represented by royal categories even among the theologians of Alexandria. But the designation of Christ as King is never eschatological. The kingship of Christ is not primarily related to his coming to earth in accordance with the prophets of the Scriptures, but to his position as the eternal, preexistent Logos. It is worth noting that second-century Christians such as Justin or Irenaeus seldom use royal categories when speaking about the Logos. Instead, they tend to reserve the royal titles for the incarnate Christ as the promised Messiah. In contrast, in Origen's theology, the messianic themes are pressed into the background, whereas the concept of the kingship of Christ is treated as secondary. In fact, Origen effects a "democratization" of the concept of the kingship by designating Christians as a royal people, a people of kings, whereas Christ is called "the King of kings."[29] In his homily on Judges, Origen says (*Hom. Judic.* 6.3):

It makes you a king over all things if Christ rules in you, for a king comes to rule. Thus if the spirit rules in you and your body obeys, if you place the lusts of the flesh beneath the yoke of rule, if you govern your sins even harder with the reins of your temperance, you shall have the right to be called king, since you are able to rule yourself aright. When you have been made thus, you shall worthily have been called as king to hear the divine words.[30]

In these words we find the messianic concept of kingship fundamentally transformed into an existential, mystical interpretation that may parallel the bride-bridegroom mysticism that he develops in his *Commentary on the Song of Songs*.[31]

The Messianic Kingdom:
Chiliasm in Early Christianity

The Jewish Apocalyptic Heritage

The most marked expression of messianism in the early centuries of Christian history, besides the arsenal of metaphors and titles that were derived from the Scriptures and perhaps also inspired by contemporary messianic Judaism, is the much-debated phenomenon of chiliasm, or millennialism. This doctrine, which entails the hope for a blissful messianic kingdom established in this present world sometime in the future to last for a thousand years, is commonly described as being very widespread in earliest Christianity, particularly in the second and early third centuries when it was advocated by prominent Christian figures, such as Justin Martyr, Irenaeus, and Tertullian. Yet during the third and fourth centuries, chiliastic ideas were pushed aside and increasingly denied legitimacy within the orthodox framework. The tension still remained in the late imperial period between those who held fast to the earthly hopes of a future messianic millennium and those who, like Jerome in the early fifth century, rejected Christian chiliasts as Judaizers who dreamt of the restoration of the earthly Jerusalem and the reestablishment of the Jewish law, including participation in the sacrificial cult, circumcision, and observance of the Sabbath. Though the chiliasts themselves were pushed into the background, they continued to provoke exegetical polemics from the fathers of the amillennialist Christian mainstream. During the late imperial and medieval periods, chiliasm was completely excluded from the further development of Christian eschatological reflection. In early modern Protestantism, however, chiliast views reemerged and gained significance in the eighteenth and nineteenth centuries, especially in the United States. Today, chiliasm is held by a number of Christian movements and sects. It finds particular emphasis in Mormonism, Seventh-day Adventism, and the Jehovah's Witnesses and is widely supported in fundamentalist Evangelicalism, to a large degree in its dispensational form.

The foundation for Christian chiliasm is an eschatological interpretation of Rev 20:1–6, which describes the binding of Satan for a period of a thousand years and the thousand-year reign of the martyrs with Christ for the same period of time. As proof texts for the chiliast hope, messianic and apocalyptic passages in the Old Testament prophecies, such as those found in Isaiah and Ezekiel, also are employed. Most likely composed in Asia Minor near the end of Emperor Domitian's reign (around 95–96 CE), Revelation can be considered as the earliest attestation of a Christian chiliast tradition. In the earliest centuries, it seems to have been particularly nurtured in Christian communities in western Asia Minor. This part of the Roman Empire had long been a stronghold of Diaspora Jewish communities, marked by far-reaching involvement and integration in Gentile culture and society rather than by introversion and isolation. The nonsectarian and integrative character of the Jewish communities in Asia Minor did not provide fertile soil for the creation of Jewish apocalyptic literature before the fall of Jerusalem in 70 CE. Except for the Jewish substratum of *Sibylline Oracles* Books 1 and 2, which most likely originated in Phrygia in the first century CE before the fall of Jerusalem and which contain an eschatological vision of the reestablishment of an earthly kingdom of the Hebrews (*Sib. Or.* 2.154–176), the Jews in Asia Minor appear to have showed little predilection for the creation of apocalyptic literature. This situation clearly poses problems for any attempt to trace a genealogy of the prophetic-apocalyptic and chiliast tendency commonly associated with Christianity in Asia Minor in the first and second centuries CE. The significance of apocalyptic and chiliastic visions for early Asiatic Christianity has been explained against the background of a long history of ecstatic cults in Asia Minor and latent hostility toward the Roman empire in the region that is claimed to have given rise to sectarian and world-rejecting prophetic movements. Yet these explanations seem rather forced and insufficient to account for this still-unsettled question, largely because they presuppose continuity where there may be none.

Revelation thus appears to be an anomaly in the context of Asia Minor Judaism. In fact, its author, John of Patmos, a member of the Jesus movement who possessed a solid Jewish identity, was doubtless of Palestinian origin, and the literary context of his apocalypse is mainly that of Palestinian Jewish apocalyptic traditions. Particularly two apocalyptic texts from this tradition were recognized as closely linked to Revelation, namely 4 *Ezra* and 2 *Baruch*.[32] Both these texts were supposedly composed in the late first century, after 70 CE, and they are both thematically reflected in John's apocalypse. We find, for instance, in 4 *Ezra* (7:26–28) a lucid parallel to the messianic and chiliast passages in Rev 20:1–6:

> For behold, the time will come, when the signs which I have foretold to you will come to pass; the city which now is not seen shall appear, and the land which now is hidden shall be disclosed. And everyone who has been delivered from the evils that I have foretold shall see my wonders. For my son the Messiah shall be revealed with those who are with him, and those who remain shall rejoice four hundred years.[33]

The text in 4 *Ezra* then reveals that when the period of earthly bliss ends, the Messiah and all who draw human breath will die, and the earth will be left in silence, desolate and empty. This will be the state of the earth until, seven days later, a new world will emerge, and the dead will rise for judgment. Later in the text (12:32–34), the role of the Messiah in the establishment of the earthly kingdom that will last for four hundred years is further specified:

> [T]his is the Messiah whom the Most High has kept until the end of days, who will arise from the posterity of David, and will come and speak to them; he will denounce them for their ungodliness and for their wickedness, and will cast up before them their contemptuous dealings. For first he will set them living before his judgment seat, and when he has reproved them, then he will destroy them. But he will deliver in mercy the remnant of my people, those who have been saved throughout my borders, and he will make them joyful until the end comes, the day of judgment, of which I spoke to you at the beginning.

The text expresses an unambiguous expectation of a Davidic king-Messiah, who will bring vengeance upon the wicked and lead the righteous into a joyful life in the future messianic kingdom that will last until the days of judgment. Against the immediate background of the catastrophe of 70 CE, *4 Ezra* thus provides to the present distress an eschatological solution of future hope, deeply rooted in a messianic interpretation of the law and the prophets.

In *2 Baruch*, written sometime between 70 and 132 CE, but describing the time of the Babylonian conquest of 587 BCE and reflecting Jewish apocalyptic sentiments after the fall of the second temple, we find striking messianic motifs shared by the more or less contemporary Revelation. The main purpose of *2 Baruch* is clearly that of consolation in times of national catastrophe. Baruch is stricken by grief after the destruction of Jerusalem and questions the benevolence of God. God replies that the present destruction is only temporary and that history merely unfolds God's providential plan. Everything that happens was predetermined by God, even the fall of Jerusalem, but also the emergence of a heavenly Jerusalem, which marks the end of history. However, in advance of this heavenly Jerusalem, there will appear an earthly Jerusalem; a messianic kingdom will emerge where the earth will bear fruit abundantly (*2 Bar.* 29:5–8):

> And on one vine will be a thousand branches, and one branch will produce a thousand clusters, and one cluster will produce a thousand grapes, and one grape will produce a cor of wine. And those who are hungry will enjoy themselves and they will, moreover, see marvels every day. For winds will go out in front of me every morning to bring the fragrance of aromatic fruits and clouds at the end of the day to distill the dew of health. And it will happen at that time that the treasury of manna will come down again from on high, and they will eat of it in those years because these are they who will have arrived at the consummation of time.[34]

The rise of this temporary kingdom of glory and bliss will bring punishment and vengeance to the wicked. The evil nations and the enemies of Zion will be utterly destroyed (39:3–40:2; 72), whereas the righteous inhabitants of the kingdom will live in bounty and peace, not afflicted by diseases, untimely deaths, envy, hatred, and painful childbirth (73; 74). Thus, those who follow the law will be given partial justification for previous troubles until the resurrection and the final judgment.

This is not the place to discuss the generic relation between *4 Ezra, 2 Baruch,* and Revelation. It suffices to observe that, in relation to earlier and contemporary Jewish apocalyptic literature, Revelation brings little that is new to the thematic patterns of that literary tradition, except for the central role of Jesus Christ in the eschatological scenario.

Papias

It is beyond doubt that the chiliast apocalyptic vision of *4 Ezra* and *2 Baruch* found its way into early Christian eschatological reflection and influenced Christian chiliast views. The most evident testimony of an immediate linkage between Jewish apocalyptic and Christian thought in post-apostolic times is connected to Papias, the early-second-century bishop of Hierapolis, who is one of the earliest Christian writers outside the New Testament to hold the belief in an earthly millennial kingdom. Toward the end of the second century, in his *Against Heresies*, Irenaeus recorded a passage from Papias, which bears close resemblance to the above-cited words from *2 Baruch* concerning the fruitfulness of the future messianic kingdom (*Haer.* 5.33.3):

> The days will come, in which vines shall grow, each having ten thousand branches, and in each branch ten thousand twigs, and in each true twig ten thousand shoots, and in each one of the shoots ten thousand clusters, and on every one of the clusters ten thousand grapes, and every grape when pressed will give five and twenty metretes of wine. And when any one of the saints shall lay hold of a cluster, another shall cry out, "I am a better cluster, take me; bless the Lord through me." In like manner [the Lord declared] that a grain of wheat would produce ten thousand ears, and that every ear should have ten thousand grains, and every grain would yield ten pounds of clear, pure, fine flour; and that all other fruit-bearing trees, and seeds and grass, would produce in similar proportions; and that all animals

feeding [only] on the productions of the earth, should [in those days] become peaceful and harmonious among each other, and be in perfect subjection to man.[35]

From Irenaeus, we learn that these words represented a tradition preserved from the "elders," who allegedly had heard it from a certain John, identified by Irenaeus as the disciple of Jesus, and who in turn had received it from Jesus. Irenaeus further notes that Papias not only heard John but also was a companion of Polycarp of Smyrna and that his account of the coming goods of the future millennial kingdom was included in the fourth volume of a collection in five volumes of circulating oral traditions about Jesus and the disciples not recorded in the New Testament. Eusebius of Caesarea in his *Church History* reveals the title of this work as *Exposition of the Words of the Lord* but conveys straightforwardly his view of the author as a man "of very limited understanding" (*Hist. eccl.* 3.39.13), an opinion clearly founded on his low assessment of Papias's chiliasm. In his report on Papias, Eusebius delivers a short but outspoken critique against Papias on account of his promotion of the teaching of the millennial kingdom (*Hist. eccl.* 3.39.11–12):

> The same writer gives also other accounts which he says came to him through unwritten tradition, certain strange parables and teachings of the Saviour, and some other more mythical things. To these belong his statement that there will be a period of some thousand years after the resurrection of the dead, and that the kingdom of Christ will be set up in material form on this very earth. I suppose he got these ideas through a misunderstanding of the apostolic accounts, not perceiving that the things said by them were spoken mystically in figures.

Eusebius accuses Papias of having led many Christian authors, including Irenaeus, into the chiliast error because of his reputation as being one of the earliest writers in the post-apostolic period. He also criticizes the conclusion made by Irenaeus concerning the identity of John with the disciple of Jesus, from whom Papias's elders received the teaching of the millennial kingdom. Instead, Eusebius identifies John with John the Elder, who Papias himself in a passage quoted by Eusebius speaks of as one of his informants (John the Disciple being another) about the oral traditions from Jesus. Though it should be noted that Papias himself never claims to have had any personal acquaintance either with John the Disciple or with John the Elder, Eusebius appears as the first Christian writer to seriously undermine an apostolic foundation and authority for Papias's chiliast belief and its reception within Christian eschatological reflection.

What the chiliast fragments from Papias make evident is the presence of a chiliast Christian tradition in Asia Minor that seems closely linked to Jewish apocalyptic eschatology as expressed in *4 Ezra* and *2 Baruch*. We do not know whether Papias was Jewish or Gentile, but his views may reflect the eschatological hopes of Jewish converts who after the Bar Kokhba revolt had moved to Asia Minor, carrying with them a nationalist apocalyptic tradition formed by decades of experiences of rebellion and oppression. Another possibility may be that the early-second-century chiliasm represented in Papias's authorship mirrors an increasing dialogue between Christians and Jews in Asia Minor, reflected in Justin's *Dialogue with Trypho*. Whatever the underlying historical, cultural, and social processes, the chiliasm of Papias may be considered as evidence for a continuous influence of contemporary Judaism on early Christianity.

Dualistic Chiliasm

Among the early Christian figures in Asia Minor of the post-apostolic era, we also find Papias's older contemporary, the elusive Cerinthus, active at the turn of the second century and claimed by early Christian sources to be both a Gnostic and a Judaic chiliast. According to Irenaeus, Cerinthus's life course once crossed with that of John, the beloved disciple of Jesus. In connection with a report on Polycarp, Irenaeus tells about an unexpected encounter between John and Cerinthus at the bathhouse in Ephesus (*Haer.* 3.3.4):

> There are also those who heard from him [i.e. Polycarp] that John, the disciple of the Lord, going to bathe at Ephesus, and perceiving Cerinthus within, rushed out of the bathhouse without bathing, exclaiming, "Let us fly, lest even the bathhouse fall down, because Cerinthus, the enemy of the truth, is within."

Irenaeus claims that John composed his Gospel against Cerinthus and the likes of him and quotes the prologue of that Gospel as immediately directed against the Gnostic doctrines, which he believes were promoted by Cerinthus. Though Irenaeus provides us with the earliest preserved information on Cerinthus, we should not take these statements as an accurate account of his teaching. In fact, the patristic testimonies about his doctrines are full of ambiguous and conflicting reports from which we should be careful not to draw hasty conclusions. Gaius of Rome in the early third century gives us a completely different picture when he describes Cerinthus not as a Gnostic, but as a chiliast, and also attributes to him the authorship of Revelation (quoted in Eusebius, *Hist. eccl.* 3.28.2.):

> But Cerinthus also, by means of revelations which he pretends were written by a great apostle, brings before us marvelous things which he falsely claims were shown him by angels; and he says that after the resurrection the kingdom of Christ will be set up on earth, and that the flesh dwelling in Jerusalem will

again be subject to desires and pleasures. And being an enemy of the Scriptures of God, he asserts, with the purpose of deceiving men, that there is to be a period of a thousand years for marriage festivals.

The image of Cerinthus as a chiliast is confirmed by the third-century Alexandrine bishop Dionysius, who rejected the attribution of Revelation to Cerinthus. It seems that for Dionysius, the chiliast view of Cerinthus was merely a consequence of his "Judaizing" tendency (*Hist. eccl.* 3.28.4–5):

> For the doctrine which he taught was this: that the kingdom of Christ will be an earthly one. And as he was himself devoted to the pleasures of the body and altogether sensual in his nature, he dreamed that that kingdom would consist in those things which he desired, namely, in the delights of the belly and of sexual passion, that is to say, in eating and drinking and marrying, and in festivals and sacrifices and the slaying of victims, under the guise of which he thought he could indulge his appetites with a better grace.

There is no indication in these accounts that supports Irenaeus's picture of Cerinthus as a Gnostic. In the eyes of Gaius and Dionysius, the heresy of Cerinthus was that of chiliasm, though for Dionysius this heresy was closely related to his "Judaizing" teaching. Thus there are in the patristic portrayal of Cerinthus two conflicting traditions that have divided modern scholars into two camps: those who believe that Cerinthus was an early Gnostic, and those who regard him as a chiliast, or in the words of A. Harnack, "a speculative Jewish Christian." Recently, C. Hill has suggested a solution to the two different traditions, taking them both into account but combining them by means of establishing an analogy between the views of Cerinthus and that of another, the second-century heresiarch Marcion.[36]

Marcion taught a fundamental separation between the highest heavenly God, who is a God of love, and the inferior God of the Hebrew Scriptures, the wrathful creator of the world. He also promoted the idea of two different Messiahs, one whose advent had been announced by the Creator-God to the prophets of the Old Testament, and one already sent by the previously unknown heavenly God, namely Jesus Christ.[37] Marcion thus acknowledged, contrary to his fellow Christians, that the Jews were right in expecting a Messiah of their own, a deliverer sent by their inferior Creator-God. The advent of this Messiah was to take place sometime in the future, exactly as announced by the Old Testament prophets, and at his coming, he would restore for the Jews the messianic land of the promise. However, this Jewish pseudo-Messiah would only provide earthly and temporal salvation for the Jews, whereas the true and heavenly Messiah, Jesus, has come to save all mankind from the boundaries of the material world.[38] It seems reasonable to consider this view as an early stage of the emergence within the Christian tradition of the Antichrist myth, later developed, for instance, by Irenaeus and Hippolytus, who specifically linked the rise of the Antichrist to the tribe of Dan.[39]

Hill argues convincingly that Marcion's teaching on the two Messiahs not only had its background in the vitality of Jewish messianism during the Jewish Wars in the first and second centuries CE, but that Marcion's view actually derived from Cerinthus.[40] Not only do we learn from Irenaeus that Cerinthus separated a higher, unknown God from the lower deity who created the world,[41] but that he also seems to have taught the existence of a Messiah other than Jesus, namely the one promised by the prophets of the Old Testament.[42] The conclusion then would be that Cerinthus, in the same way as Marcian, acknowledged the rise of a Jewish millennial kingdom, ruled by a Jewish Messiah as predicted in the Hebrew Scriptures. This conclusion is particularly well supported by the report of Gaius quoted previously. Given this background, it does not seem far-fetched to suggest that Dionysius of Alexandria's assessment of Cerinthus as a Judaizing heretic was based on Cerinthus's vision of the restored Jewish messianic kingdom, implying the reinstatement of the temple, its sacrifices, and other Jewish cultic practices.

The Case of the New Prophecy

From Asia Minor also sprang the so-called Montanist movement, known as the "New Prophecy," founded in the middle of the second century CE by the Phrygian prophet Montanus, accompanied by the two prophetesses Priscilla and Maximilla. Ecstatic prophecy is thought to have been at the very core of this movement, whose leaders allegedly claimed to be guided by the active presence of the Paraclete. The lack of useful Montanist sources, however, has left us highly dependent on the tendentious reports of Eusebius, Jerome, and Epiphanius. The assumed predilection of the Montanists for ecstatic visions and oracles occupies much space in their opponents' reports. Eusebius, quoting an anonymous adversary of the Montanists (*Hist. eccl.* 5.16.7), tells us that Montanus:

> became beside himself, and being suddenly in a sort of frenzy and ecstasy, he raved, and began to babble and utter strange things, prophesying in a manner contrary to the constant custom of the Church handed down by tradition from the beginning.

One of the most notable testimonies concerning the prophetic visions of the Montanists comes from Epiphanius (*Pan.* 49.1):

> For the Quintillians or Priscillians say that in Pepuza, either Quintilla or Priscilla (I cannot say for sure

which), at any rate one of them as I was saying was
sleeping in Pepuza and Christ came to her and slept
by her in the following way, as she in her error
relates: "Christ came to me in the form of a woman,
dressed in a bright robe, and placed in me wisdom
and revealed to me that this place is holy and that
here the Jerusalem from heaven is coming down.[43]

Scholars in the nineteenth and twentieth centuries generally considered this passage from Epiphanius as conclusive
evidence that Montanism essentially was a chiliast movement. In recent years, however, this assumption has come
under increasing scrutiny. The reason for this relates largely
to the fact that chiliasm does not appear as an issue in eccle-
siastical refutation of the Montanists, something which
would be expected if chiliasm had been recognized as a
central element in the Montanist teaching. Neither do any
of the preserved prophetic oracles provide clear proof for
chiliast views within the movement. Epiphanius's report
about the vision of Priscilla or Quintilla, moreover, appears
too vague for an obvious conclusion considering a Montanist expectation of a future millennium. What can be
derived from the passage is merely a biased testimony
claiming that Montanists held a doctrine of a heavenly
Jerusalem descending to earth and that this descent takes
place, or will take place, "here" (*hōde*), most likely implying the Asia Minor town of Pepuza.

At least from what is told about them by their opponents,
we may conclude that the followers of the Prophecy seem
to have been rather preoccupied with thoughts of Jerusalem. Eusebius quotes the Christian writer Apollonius,
relating that the two small Phrygian towns of Pepuza and
Tymion were named Jerusalem by Montanus in his desire
to gather people to them from everywhere.[44] Given that we
trust these two sources on Montanist preoccupation with
Jerusalem, we may ask if this concern is related to an eschatological promise in the future, developed from the Apoc-

alypse of John or other apocalyptic texts such as 4 *Ezra*. Nothing in the preserved sources indicates that this would be the case. In fact, the apocalyptic-millennialist hope commonly associated with the Montanist movement seems completely absent. Instead, from the report of Apollonius that Pepuza already was given the name Jerusalem, it appears that we are dealing with a more realized kind of eschatology, focusing not so much on the place itself, but on the prophetic people who inhabited that place. The notion of Jerusalem descending from heaven was not a messianic kingdom to be realized in the future, but rather a manifestation of true discipleship in the present.[45]

Chiliasm among the Orthodox

The Jewish hope for possession of the promised land received a fatal blow with the defeat of the Bar Kokhba revolt. But what the restored Israel under Simon Bar Kokhba essentially demonstrated was that for contemporary mainstream Judaism, there was nothing "spiritualized" about the vision of the messianic kingdom. Jewish messianism was essentially a political movement with a physically tangible aim: the restoration of the independence of the state of Israel.[46] After decades of dealing with Jewish troublemakers, Roman authorities certainly had learned to treat expressions of such national aspirations with much concern. The attempt of Emperor Hadrian to expel Jews from Judaea and turn Jerusalem into the pagan city of Aelia Capitolina was a desperate manifestation of the anxiety, which for generations had seized the Roman authorities, over the rise within the empire of an independent Jewish kingdom. However, as late as the mid-second century, Roman anxiety over the political and military consequences of Jewish messianism seems to have been directed against Christians as well. In his *First Apology*, written about 155 CE, Justin Martyr provides the following defense to Roman suspicion about nationalist messianism among Christians (*1 Apol.* 11):

> And when you hear that we look for a kingdom, you suppose, without making any inquiry, that we speak of a human kingdom; whereas we speak of that which is with God, as appears also from the confession of their faith made by those who are charged with being Christians, though they know that death is the punishment awarded to him who so confesses. For if we looked for a human kingdom, we should also deny our Christ, that we might not be slain; and we should strive to escape detection, that we might obtain what we expect. But since our thoughts are not fixed on the present, we are not concerned when men cut us off; since also death is a debt which must at all events be paid.[47]

This passage appears as a definite rejection of the notion of an earthly messianic kingdom. The kingdom does not belong to the present world but rather is to be considered as a state with God (*meta theou*) in heaven. This heavenly state will be attained immediately at death, at least for those who demonstrated readiness to give up their earthly life for the sake of Christ. This will be the reward for those who care little for material things and ambitions in the present and instead desire to enter the celestial realm to be with God.

Yet we find in the writings of Justin one of the most evident cases of chiliasm among second-century Christian writers, and from which it is made clear that he in fact embraces the notion of a peaceful era of a thousand years, followed by a universal resurrection and the last judgment. This expressed chiliasm is found in chapters 80–81 of the *Dialogue with Trypho* (written after the *First Apology*), where we learn that a millennial kingdom will take place in a restored Jerusalem (*Dial.* 80):

> But I and others, who are right-minded Christians on all points, are assured that there will be a resurrection of the dead, and a thousand years in Jerusalem, which will then be built, adorned, and enlarged, [as] the prophets Ezekiel and Isaiah and others declare.[48]

Some scholars seem to disregard the existence in Justin's writings of these two conflicting eschatological approaches, presenting instead Justin's eschatological teaching as one integrated system; whereas others recognize the inconsistency in his eschatological thinking. It is possible to explain the two different views as the result of a personal development of opinion between the writing of the *First Apology* and the *Dialogue*. Another solution may be that the *Dialogue* is composed of a record of a real debate in which Justin did not participate. However, we do not have any indication in the text that suggests that the opinions expressed by the opponent of Trypho are not Justin's own.

Justin claims that he is not alone in holding a chiliast opinion and demonstrates clearly his awareness that although he is not alone in this opinion, there are many among orthodox Christians who do not share his chiliast views. Among those who do not accept the view of the millennial kingdom, he mentions those "who are called Christians, but are godless, impious heretics." These words resemble the words of Irenaeus (*Haer.* 5.31.1):

> Since, again, some who are reckoned among the orthodox go beyond the pre-arranged plan for the exaltation of the just, and are ignorant of the methods by which they are disciplined beforehand for incorruption, they thus entertain heretical opinions. For the heretics, despising the handiwork of God, and not admitting the salvation of their flesh, while they also treat the promise of God

contemptuously, and pass beyond God altogether in the sentiments they form, affirm that immediately upon their death they shall pass above the heavens and the Demiurge, and go to the Mother or to that Father whom they have feigned. Those persons, therefore, who disallow a resurrection affecting the whole man, and as far as in them lies remove it from the midst, how can they be wondered at, if again they know nothing as to the plan of the resurrection?

Thus, in Irenaeus's view, there were Christians who could be considered orthodox but, nevertheless, failed to acknowledge the necessity of the future establishment of an earthly millennium. For Irenaeus, these Christians, orthodox at least by name, thus shared their views with heretics such as the Valentinian Gnostics and others who denied the possibility for the material body to be saved, since these so-called orthodox Christians believed that righteous souls at death immediately entered the heavenly realm.

In the fifth book of *Against Heresies*, Irenaeus thus positioned himself outright as a chiliast. There has been a noticeable tendency among modern scholars to downplay or even ignore this aspect of his theology. Writers who give the chiliast views of Irenaeus serious consideration often suggest that Irenaeus's belief in an earthly millennium is to be regarded primarily as a natural, and therefore understandable and excusable, consequence of his ardent anti-Gnosticism. Yet it must be recognized that Irenaeus did not simply adopt from Asia Minor a millennialist tradition resting solidly on first-century Jewish apocalypticism. He seems, rather, to have effected a thorough transformation of earlier millennial expectations, and perhaps, in doing so, contributed to the marginalization of messianic chiliasm in late antique and medieval Christianity.

C. R. Smith has shown that there are three essential features in Irenaeus's teaching on the paradisal millennium that clearly set him apart from the earlier chiliast tradition. First, Irenaeus's notion of the millennial paradise does not appear as a literary millennium in the sense of what is revealed in Rev 20:1–6. Irenaeus bases his idea of the millennium completely on Genesis and the six days of creation, each day being a thousand years, and identifies the millennium with the seventh day, the Sabbath of the Lord. Thus a restored earthly paradise will appear six thousand years after the creation. Yet we do not find in the text any definition of the exact time span of the earthly paradise. Second, Irenaeus's lack of interest in the actual time period of the restored paradise is associated with this view on the fundamental purpose of the paradisal millennium: "the kingdom . . . is the commencement of incorruption, by means of which . . . those who shall be worthy are accustomed gradually to partake of the divine nature" (*Haer.* 5.32.1).[49]

Thus the purpose of the earthly millennium is to prepare the righteous for the final salvation. Consequently, the duration of the millennium has not been decided according to a hidden plan of God, but depends entirely on the spiritual progress of the individual. Third, since the duration of the millennium depends on the progressing efforts and spiritual maturity of the individual soul, there is no sharp dividing line between the millennium and the new heaven and earth, timeless and uncorrupted. The creation will never perish but will continue to be inhabited by the resurrected. The least worthy of these renewed individuals will live in a restored Jerusalem, whereas the more worthy will enter the paradise on the new earth, which seems to be a place between heaven and earth. The most worthy, the saints, will enter heaven and unite with God. This vision of the eschatological realities cannot be separated from Irenaeus's teaching of recapitulation, the heavily emphasized need for full restoration of the earthly paradise for the purpose of bringing believers to full spiritual maturity and likeness with God.

What we find in the eschatological theology of Irenaeus is a radical divergence from the notion of the messianic millennium of *4 Ezra, 2 Baruch,* and Rev 20–21. For Irenaeus, the eschatological kingdom has nothing to do with reward or consolation, but is instead intimately and inseparably connected with his unified conception of salvation history. Paradoxically, the chiliast teaching of Irenaeus seems to point toward the development of non-chiliast theology of the mystical union with God through a process of gradual deification or divinization, a view that finds most profound expression in the Eastern Christian tradition.

One early critic of Christian chiliasm was Celsus. Though Celsus himself does not mention chiliasm explicitly in the preserved fragments of his *On the True Doctrine,* it is clear that Origen in the *Contra Celsum* understands Celsus's words against that background. When Celsus puts the following question into the mouths of the Christians, "Where do we hope to go after death?", Celsus himself replies on behalf of the Christians he is mocking: "To another land better than this." And then he makes the comment that even the great men of the past spoke of a happy life reserved for the souls of the blessed, whether they called it "the island of the blessed" or "Elusion" (*Cels.* 7.28). For those Christians who had read Plato's *Phaedo,* writes Celsus, it should be clear that even there a "land" is mentioned where the immortal souls will go after the death of the body. Origen understands Celsus's words as a critique against the idea of a life-after-death promise that concerns a much better and more excellent place on the earth than any place known to the living. Origen blames Celsus for not noticing that Moses, who predates the Greek literature, spoke of a land promised by God (*Cels.* 7.28):

> Moses, who is much older than the Greek literature, introduces God as promising to those who lived according to His law the holy land, which is "a good

land and a large, a land flowing with milk and honey;" which promise is not to be understood to refer, as some suppose, to that part of the earth which we call Judea; for it, however good it may be, still forms part of the earth, which was originally cursed for the transgression of Adam.

By means of the argument that the earth is cursed as a result of Adam's transgression, Origen thus explicitly rejects the idea of the Holy Land as being the good land promised by God to the righteous. Therefore, the Promised Land, according to Origen, must be located somewhere else, not on earth but in heaven (*Cels.* 7.29):

Judea and Jerusalem were the shadow and figure of that pure land, goodly and large, in the pure region of heaven, in which is the heavenly Jerusalem. And it is in reference to this Jerusalem that the apostle spoke, as one who, "being risen with Christ, and seeking those things which are above," had found a truth which formed no part of the Jewish mythology. "Ye are come," says he, "unto Mount Sion, and unto the city of the living God, the heavenly Jerusalem, and to an innumerable company of angels."

According to Origen, Christian chiliasts revealed themselves as understanding the Scriptures according to what he calls a "Jewish" sense, since they "[were] drawing from them nothing worthy of the divine promises" (*Princ.* 2.11.2).[50] Whereas Origen accuses the chiliasts of being absorbed by physical rather than spiritual desires through their dreams of an earthly messianic kingdom, there is, as R. Wilken has noted, also a christological dimension in his anti-chiliasm. Origen's criticism of chiliasm is clearly linked with a defense of an orthodox, non-chiliast Christian messianism. If the chiliasts were right and the fulfillment of the prophetic oracles concerning the Promised Land was still to come, that would mean that the prophecies of the Scriptures were not fulfilled through the coming of Christ and that the messianic era had not yet occurred. However, if Christ really was the Messiah, all prophecies should have been fulfilled, and the hope for an earthly Jerusalem could not be considered as anything but completely vain. Thus, a spiritual interpretation of the promises of the Holy Land was necessary if the Christian belief in Jesus as the Messiah was to be maintained.[51]

Conclusion

Much of the prestige attached to religions in the Roman world was derived from the assurance of their ancientness. Supernatural truth was identified on the basis of tradition, and religions that had no tradition or roots easily became objects of ridicule. The apparent novelty of the Christian faith, in the eyes of the Romans, brought grave discredit upon the Christian claim of exclusive possession of divine truth. The accusation that Christians lacked antiquity was countered by Christians, who asserted that the Christian faith, though it emerged not earlier than during the reign of Tiberius, was indeed founded upon sacred documents far more ancient than anything written in Greek or Latin. Not only was the dependence of Christianity on the Hebrew Scriptures affirmed, but it was also demonstrated that the justification of Christianity rested on the fulfillment of the ancient Jewish prophecies in Jesus Christ. Thus, messianism was the fundament for the justification and credibility of Christianity among the Romans as a religion worthy of acknowledgment and respect.

Messianism, of course, also was at the heart of the conflict between Christians and Jews. With the emergence of a specifically Christian interpretation of the Old Testament, messianic promises, and the Jewish rejection of these same promises, the Jewish-Christian conflict became completely focused on the Christian claim that Jesus Christ was the Messiah promised by the Scriptures. The Jews certainly did not lack counterarguments to the Christian claims, and some of them undoubtedly are recorded in Justin's *Dialogue with Trypho*. Remarkably, some Jewish arguments against the messiahship of Jesus also were used by the pagan Celsus, criticizing the Christians for claiming as the Messiah a person who lacked the most important messianic quality, namely that of kingship. Origen's reply to the objections of Celsus demonstrates an evident shift in the reception of messianism in early Christianity. Instead of reflecting upon the messianic proof texts from the Old Testament in terms of the traditional Jewish imagery of messianic kingship, the principal interest is now turned to Christ as the eternal and preexistent Word. Through his transformation of messianism into Christology, Origen contributes in setting the scene for the trinitarian and Christological reflection in the fourth and fifth centuries.

Although it probably is an exaggeration to claim the dominance of the chiliast doctrine in the first and second centuries, we can nevertheless consider this belief as one significant eschatological trend in the early Christian church. Chiliasm in the early church appears as a tradition mainly connected to Asia Minor, where we find the first obvious evidence of chiliasm in the Christian tradition, namely in Revelation. It is clear that this text rests firmly on Jewish apocalyptic tradition, represented especially by *4 Ezra* and *2 Baruch*. To this tradition we may also connect Papias, whose teaching on the fruitfulness of the millennial kingdom seems to have been derived from *2 Baruch*. Early apocalyptic reflection also was employed in the dualistic systems of Cerinthus and Marcion, both of whom seem to have held the view of an earthly kingdom belonging to the Jews, whereas the true righteous souls will enter the heavenly kingdom. However, a more "orthodox" form of chiliasm is revealed in the works of Justin and Irenaeus,

whose chiliast views sometimes have been taken as affirmation of the dominance of millennial hope in ante-Nicene
Christianity. With Irenaeus we experience a fundamental
transformation of the messianic chiliasm of Jewish apocalypticism in terms of a new emphasis on the close relationship between salvation, transfiguration, perfection, and
deification, achieved through a gradual progress of personal growth and maturing. These were themes that
formed the foundation for the development of Christian
mystical and ascetical theology, which would, at the end,
render the hopes for a future earthly messianic kingdom
fatally obsolete.

GLOSSARY

Amoraic period, named after the rabbis living ca 200–450 CE who were called *Amoraim* (lit. "sayers" or "recounters"). During this period the main part of the rabbinic writings, known as Amoraic literature, was composed.

Apocalypticism, from Greek, *apokalypsis*, "an uncovering, a revelation," the idea that God has revealed the future in which evil forces will be defeated and God's kingdom will be established. The Book of Daniel, *4 Ezra*, *1 Enoch*, and Revelation are examples of *apocalypses*, "revelations." Apocalyptic literature can also be found among the Dead Sea Scrolls.

Asia Minor, the broad peninsula between the Black and the Mediterranean Seas, which today constitutes the Asian part of modern Turkey.

Bar Kokhba, (Simeon Bar Kosba), Jewish leader who led a revolt against the Romans in 132–135 (the second Jewish war). The most prominent rabbi of the time, R. Akiva, considered Simeon Bar Kosba to be the Messiah and gave him the title Bar Kokhba, "Son of the Star" (after Num. 24:17). In 135 he was killed in his stronghold, Betar, in Jerusalem.

Babylonian Talmud, see Talmud

Celsus, second half of the second century CE, Greek Platonic philosopher and polemicist against the Christian religion during the reign of Marcus Aurelius; author of the anti-Christian treatise *Alēthēs logos* (*On* *the True Doctrine*), which is preserved through extensive quotes in Origen's *Contra Celsum* (written perhaps in 248).

Cerinthus, ca 100 CE, early Christian contemporary of Polycarp in Ephesus; first mentioned by Irenaeus who describes him as a Gnostic heretic, whereas Eusebius records him as a Judaizing chiliast. His teaching is commonly described as a mix between Gnosticism and Judaizing Christianity.

Chiliasm, from Greek, *chiliasmos*, "a thousand years," also *millennialism*, the idea of a messianic kingdom of peace and righteousness which will be established in this present world upon the second coming of Christ.

Clement of Alexandria (Titus Flavius Clements), ca 150–ca 215 CE, Christian theologian and head of the catechetical school of Alexandria, author of the *Paedagogus* (*The Instructor*), the *Stromata* (*Miscellanies*), and *Protrepticus* (*Exhortation to the Greeks*). He followed Philo in blending biblical tradition with Greek philosophy, undertaking allegorical interpretations of biblical texts, and developing the concept of Christ as Logos incarnate.

Dead Sea Scrolls, see Qumran

Diaspora, from Greek *diaspora* ("dispersion"), designation of the Jewish population that lived outside the Land of Israel. The first important Jewish Diaspora was the result of the Babylonian exile in the 6th century BCE. During the first century CE, large Jewish groups (about 7–10 percent of the whole population) could be found in Alexandria, Antioch-on-the-Orontes, and Rome.

Dio Cassius (Cassius Dio Cocceianus), ca 155–ca 235 CE, Greco-Roman politician and historian; author of *Rōmaika*, written in Greek and covering Roman history from the landing of Aeneas in Italy after the fall of Troy to 229 CE.

Dispensationalism, a Christian eschatological doctrine first developed by Plymouth Brethren leader John Nelson Darby (1800–1882), characterized by its division of history into several separate dispensations or ages in which God's truth and will has been revealed progressively over time.

Elijah, a ninth century BCE Israelite prophet appearing in 1–2 Kings where he raises the dead, brings fire down from heaven, and at last ascends into heaven on a whirlwind. A prophecy in the Book of Malachi (4:5) prompted expectations of his eschatological return.

Enuma Elish (lit. "When on high," from its first words) the Babylonian creation epic (ca 8th century BCE). The main theme is the elevation of the Babylonian chief god, Marduk, above over other Mesopotamian gods. The goddess Tiamat, the personification of salt water, plans to kill the younger gods, but is defeated by Marduk, who creates the world from her body.

Epiphanius, ca 315–403, Christian ascetic and writer, bishop of Salamis in Cyprus; most known for his *Panarion* (*Medicine chest*), which is a systematic refutation of eighty heresies in three books. This work is of immense importance for our knowledge of the doctrinal diversity of earliest Christianity.

Eschatology, from Greek, *eschatos*, "last." The term is used to describe ideas about what will happen at the end of history in both Judaism and Christianity.

Eusebius of Caesarea, ca 263–ca 340 CE, often referred to as the father of church history, bishop of Caesarea in Palestine from about 313. His major work is his *Church History*, recording the history of the Christian church from Jesus to Constantine the Great and containing quotations and references to many lost early Christian writings. His vast literary production includes historical, apologetic, exegetical, and dogmatic works. He participated in the first ecumenical Council of Nicaea in 325 and subscribed to its Trinitarian decisions, but joined the opponents of the Nicene party in the further developments of the so-called Arian controversy.

Gaius (Caius), beginning of the third century CE, Christian author in Rome in the time of the Roman bishop Zephyrinus (199–217). According to Eusebius, he rejected the Johannine authorship of Revelation and attributed it instead to Cerinthus.

Galen, ca 129–ca 199 CE, Greek physician and philosopher, born in Pergamon in Asia Minor. From 162 he lived in Rome where he became a reputed physician, and served as court physician to emperors Marcus Aurelius and Commodus. He wrote extensively on anatomy, medicine and philosophy, and was still in the 19th century considered as the most prominent medical authority.

Gnosticism, from Greek *gnōsis*, "knowledge." The term is used to describe different religious movements especially during the first centuries CE. Some Christian movements were influenced by Gnostic ideas, especially the idea that the soul was trapped in the evil physical world and could only be set free and return to its divine spiritual origin by acquiring secret knowledge.

Hasmonean dynasty, in 167 BCE, the Jewish priest Mattathias and his five sons initiated a revolt against the Syrian overlords. Mattathias died soon after the revolt began; thereafter the battle was led by his son, Judas Maccabeus ("the Hammerer"). In 164 BCE Judas gained control over Jerusalem and the Temple was rededicated. During the following centuries, the Maccabeans obtained full control over the land and in 142 BCE Simon, the brother of Judas, won complete independence. Until 63 BCE, when the Romans captured Jerusalem, descendants of the Maccabees, known as the Hasmoneans (after their ancestor Hasmon), ruled the land as an autonomous state.

Hellenism, in its broadest sense, Hellenism denotes the Greek culture and ideals that spread over the ancient world as a result of the conquests of Alexander the Great. As a cultural phenomenon, the Hellenistic legacy continued well into the 6th century CE.

Hermeneutics, from Greek *hermēneuō,* "to interpret," the theory and practice of interpretation. From the time of the Reformation, hermeneutics has been understood as a method for *understanding* the biblical text and thus closely related to biblical studies; but Augustine had already created a set of rules (*ars interpretandi*) for text interpretation. In contemporary philosophy, hermeneutics denotes more broadly the study of different methods for interpreting not only texts but all systems of meaning.

Hippolytus, ca 170–ca 235 CE, Christian presbyter in Rome and opponent of the Roman bishops Zephyrinus (199–217) and Callistus (217-222). Among his voluminously works (in Greek) we find commentaries on the Prophet Daniel and on the Song of Songs, the polemical treatise *Refutation of all Heresies,* and the *Apostolic Tradition,* a church order of great importance for our knowledge about church life and liturgy in the third century.

Incarnation, from Latin *in carno,* "enfleshed," the idea that a divine being assumes human flesh.

Irenaeus, died ca 202 CE, Christian bishop of Lugdunum (Lyon). He came originally from Asia Minor and was a disciple of Polycarp. He is known as the first great theologian of the Christian church in the post-apostolic time. The most important of his work is the *Adversus Haereses* (*Against Heresies*), in which he describes different Gnostic systems and refutes them. Irenaeus is the first Christian writer who argues for the canonicity of the four Gospels.

Jerome, ca 347–420 CE, Christian biblical scholar and advocate of asceticism, known for his translation of the Bible into Latin, the *Ver-*

sio Vulgata (*Common Version*). His preserved 117 letters provide valuable knowledge to the religious situation in the Late Roman Empire.

Jerusalem Talmud, see Talmud

Josephus, (Joseph Ben Matthias/Flavius Josephus), ca 37 CE–ca 100 CE, Jewish priest, Pharisee, and historian. Josephus took part in the revolt against the Romans in 66–70, was captured, but won Vespasian's favor by prophesying that he would become emperor. After the war Josephus moved to Rome and was granted Roman citizenship, and it was here under Flavian patronage that he wrote all of his known works, *Bellum judaicum* (*Jewish War*), *Antiquitates judaicae* (*Jewish Antiquities*), *Contra Apionem* (*Against Apion*) and *Vita* (*Life*).

Justin Martyr, ca 100–ca 165 CE, Christian writer and apologist from Palestine, known for his *Apology* (in two parts) and the *Dialogue with Trypho*. Against pagan and Jewish opponents he defended Christianity as the true philosophy. He was martyred in Rome about 165 during the persecution of Christians by Marcus Aurelius. His trial is recorded in the *Acts of Justin Martyr*.

Maccabean revolt, see Hasmonean dynasty

Marcion, died ca 160 CE, Christian theologian, born in Sinope in Asia Minor. In 139 he came to Rome and joined the Christian congregation there, but was excommunicated because of his rejection of the Old Testament and his teaching of a radical separation of the God of creation from the God of salvation. Of the New Testament writings he only accepted Luke, omitting the first two chapters, and ten of the so-called Pauline letters, excluding Hebrews and the Pastoral Letters.

Marduk, see *Enuma Elish*

Melito of Sardis, died ca 180, Christian bishop of Sardis. Of his many books (Eusebius mentions 20 titles) only fragments have survived, with the exception of his homily *Peri Pascha* (*Concerning the Passover*) in which he formulated the charge of *deicide*, i.e. the idea that the Jews were responsible for the crucifixion of Jesus.

Midrash, a rabbinic method of exegesis of a biblical text. The method is based on the assumptions that the Bible is of divine origin, that it is perfect containing no contradictions, inconsistencies, or superfluity, that it is always relevant, and that there is a hidden message behind the apparent meaning. The word midrash can also refer to a compilation of biblical interpretations.

Mishnah, rabbinic oral traditions that were collected and edited ca

200 CE by Yehudah Ha-Nasi. It is thematically organized according to topic and mostly contains discussions of rabbinic law.

Millenarianism, also millennialism, from Latin, *millennium*, "thousand years." See Chiliasm.

Montanus, second century CE, Christian prophet and charismatic leader from Phrygia in Asia Minor; founder of the Montanist movement, also known as "the New Prophecy," together with the two women prophets Priscilla (or Prisca) and Maximilla.

Origen, ca 185–ca 254 CE, theologian and writer in Alexandria, known as the first great Christian exegete and the main representative of Alexandrine theology. He was one of the most prolific writers of the early Church, but as a result of later condemnations of his theology only portions of his writings have survived, mainly in Latin translations. He seems to have been the first Christian scholar to undertake the study of the Hebrew Bible, collecting six Hebrew and two Greek versions into the first critical edition of the Bible, the *Hexapla*, of which only fragments remain. He wrote a vast number of Scriptural commentaries, marked by his allegorical method of interpretation. With the *Contra Celsum*, the reply to the attacks on Christianity made by the pagan Celsus, he is sometimes ranked among the great apologists of the early Church. His most controversial work, *De Principiis*, is strongly colored by Platonist speculative philosophy, with the idea of a pre-existent fall of souls and the return of all the fallen souls to God (*apokatastasis*).

Papias, died ca 150 CE, Christian bishop of Hierapolis in Asia Minor. Irenaeus describes him as a hearer of John the disciple and a companion of Polycarp. His work, *Exposition of the Words of the Lord*, which contains oral traditions and legends concerning Jesus, is lost, but fragments are preserved in the works of Irenaeus, Eusebius, and other sources.

Pentateuch, see Torah

Philo of Alexandria, ca 25 BCE–40 CE, Jewish philosopher in Alexandria who fused Hebrew mythical thought with Greek philosophical thought. His doctrine of the Logos, employment of allegorical exegesis, and contemplative mysticism deeply influenced later Christian theology, especially in Alexandria with Clement of Alexandria and Origen.

Pliny the Younger (Gaius Plinius Caecilius Secundus), ca 62–ca 113 CE, Roman official and writer, Roman governor of Bithynia from 111–

113. His letters, collected in ten books, provide valuable information about Roman administration and every day life.

Polycarp, died ca 156 CE, Christian bishop of Smyrna in Asia Minor, said to have been a disciple of John the disciple. His *Letter to the Phillipians* survives. He was an associate with Ignatius of Antioch who addressed to him his *Letter to St. Polycarp.* The *Martyrdom of Polycarp,* recording his crucifixion and death, belongs to the first of the *Acts of the Martyrs.*

Qumran, ancient settlement located near the Dead Sea, near where the Dead Sea Scrolls were found in 1947. The settlement was constructed sometime during the reign of John Hyrcanus (134–104 BCE) and was destroyed by the Romans in 68 CE. Most scholars consider the place to have been home to a Jewish sect, possibly the Essenes, who composed some of the Scrolls; but there is no scholarly consensus concerning this. The Scrolls date from the third century BCE to 68 CE and consist mainly of biblical books, apocryphal or pseudepigraphical works, and writings regarded as pertaining to the sect who lived at Qumran.

Rabbinic Judaism, the dominant form of Judaism that developed after the destruction of Jerusalem and the Temple by the Romans in 70 CE. It is based on the tradition that the Torah revealed at Sinai had both a written and an oral form, the written being the Hebrew Bible and the oral being the rabbinic commentary on it.

Second Temple Judaism, 516 BCE–70 CE, the period during which the Temple built after the return from the Babylonian exile existed.

Septuagint, the Greek translation of the Hebrew Bible. The Septuagint is often abbreviated as LXX, from the Latin term *septuaginta* "seventy," which refers to a legend, best known from the pseudepigraphic *Letter of Aristeas,* according to which the translation was made by seventy (or seventy-two) translators. By the second century BCE all books of the Bible had been translated into Greek and the Septuagint became the form of text commonly used by Jews in the Diaspora (and eventually also by adherents to the Jesus movement).

Suetonius (Gaius Suetonius Tranquillus), ca 70–ca 140 CE, Roman historian, author of *De Vita Caesarum* (*Lives of the Caesars*), a series of twelve biographies of the emperors from Caesar to Domitian, and *De Viris Illustribus* (*On Famous Men*), of which only fragments have been preserved.

Synoptic Gospels, Mark, Matthew and Luke, so called because they share much of their subject matter and to a large extent use the same or similar wording. According to the widely accepted two-source hypothesis, the reason for this is that Matthew and Luke used Mark as their primary source.

Tacitus (Publius Cornelius Tacitus), ca 55–ca 120 CE, Roman official and historian. His writings include *Historiae* (*The Histories*) and *The Annals,* which together cover Roman history from the death of Augustus in 14 CE to the death of Domitian in 96 CE.

Talmud, a compilation that consists of the Mishnah and commentaries on it. The Talmud exists in two versions: the Jerusalem Talmud, composed by rabbis in the Land of Israel who flourished from the third to the fifth century CE, and the Babylonian Talmud, composed by Babylonian rabbis who lived from the third to the seventh century CE. The Babylonian is the more extensive version and the one more widely studied by religious Jews.

Tannaitic period, named after rabbis living ca 70–200 CE, called the Tannaim (lit., "those who learn"). During this period the main part of the rabbinic writings, known as the Tannaitic literature, was composed.

Tertullian (Quintus Septimius Florens Tertullianus), died after 220 CE, Christian theologian and writer in Carthage, North Africa. His vast literary production includes apologetics, polemic tracts against Jews, pagans, and Marcion (*Adversus Marcionem*), and practical instruction for church life. He had a deep influence on the development of the theological language of the Latin West, introducing the terms *substantia* (substance) and *persona* (person) to describe the relation between the persons in the Trinity. Tertullian joined the Montanist movement and broke with the Catholic Church in 207.

Torah, the word has three different but related meanings in Jewish tradition. In its most narrow sense it denotes the Five Books of Moses (the Pentateuch); in a broader sense it includes all of the Hebrew Bible; and in its broadest sense it refers both to the Hebrew Bible (the written Torah) and its rabbinic commentaries (oral Torah).

NOTES

1. Pre-Christian Jewish Messianism

1. On the anointing of the king, see Mettinger, *King and Messiah*, 185–232.

2. There is some evidence for the anointing of prophets in the Hebrew Bible. In 1 Kgs 19:16, Elijah is told to anoint Elisha as his successor. The prophetic speaker in Isa 61:1 says that "God has anointed me."

3. Fitzmyer, *The One Who is to Come*, 62, regards Dan 9:25 as messianic in the eschatological sense, because of "the occurrence of the word משיח [*māšîaḥ*] . . . with a temporal preposition having a future connotation," although the reference is clearly to the restoration after the exile, which was long past when the passage was written.

4. *Pace* Fitzmyer, *Dead Sea Scrolls*, 73–110.

5. Dalley, *Myths from Mesopotamia*, 228–77.

6. Wyatt, *Myths of Power*.

7. Assmann, "Die Zeugung des Sohnes" Brunner, *Die Geburt des Gottkönigs*; O'Connor and Silverman, *Ancient Egyptian Kingship*. See also the classic study of Frankfort, *Kingship and the Gods*, 15–212.

8. Machinist, "Kingship and Divinity."

9. Day, "Canaanite Inheritance," 83.

10. Keel, *Symbolism of the Biblical World*, 252–55; Koch, "Der König als Sohn Gottes," 11–15; Otto, "Psalm 2," 335–49; idem, "Politische Theologie," 33–65.

11. Roberts, "Whose Child is This?" 115–29; von Rad, "Royal Ritual," 222–31.
12. Healey, "Immortality," 245–54.
13. McCarter, *2 Samuel*, 220–21. See the fundamental studies of McCarthy, "II Samuel 7," 131–38, and Cross, *Canaanite Myth*, 248–57.
14. Mettinger, "Cui Bono?" 193–214. Schniedewind, *Society and the Promise to David*, 35–36, adopts an extreme position by dating all of 2 Sam 7:1–17, except for verses 1b and 13a, to the time of David.
15. For an overview, see Pomykala, *Davidic Dynasty*, 17–68.
16. Wegner, *Examination*; Williamson, "Messianic Texts," 244–50; idem, *Variations on a Theme*.
17. Laato, *A Star is Rising*, 123–25; Strack and Billerbeck, *Kommentar zum Neuen Testament*, 75.
18. Alt, "Jesaja 8,23–9,6," 29–49.
19. Roberts, "Whose Child is This?"
20. Duhm, *Das Buch Jesaja*, 36, described this passage as the prophet's swan song; von Rad, *Old Testament Theology* 2:169–70; Wildberger, *Isaiah 1–12*, 465–69; Williamson, "Messianic Texts," 258–64.
21. Sweeney, *Isaiah 1–39*, 204–5; idem, *King Josiah of Judah*, 321.
22. Blenkinsopp, *Isaiah 1–39*, 264: "the anticipation of a new growth from the old stock of Jesse, ancestor of the Davidic dynasty (1 Sam 16:1), aligns with dynastic aspirations that come to expression in other texts from the post-destruction period (Jer 23:5–6; 33:14–22; Ezek 37: 24–28; Amos 9:11–15; Mic 5:1–3[2–4])." The dates of several of these texts also are debated. For a list of scholars who date Isa 11:1–9 to the postexilic period, see Wildberger, *Isaiah 1–12*, 465.
23. E.g., Paul, *Amos*, 288–89; von Rad, *Old Testament Theology*, 2.138.
24. Wellhausen (*Die Kleinen Propheten*, 96) famously remarked that the passage is "roses and lavender instead of blood and iron." Blenkinsopp, *History of Prophecy*, 77; Wolff, *Joel and Amos*, 352–53.
25. Hillers, *Micah*, 64–67, defends an eighth-century date. Blenkinsopp, *History of Prophecy*, 92, regards it as postexilic.
26. Roberts, "Contribution," 46.
27. Fishbane, *Biblical Interpretation*, 471–74; Schniedewind, *Society and the Promise to David*, 135–36.
28. Joyce, "King and Messiah in Ezekiel," 323–37.
29. Levenson, *Theology*, 75–101.
30. Blenkinsopp, *History of Prophecy*, 231.
31. Hanson, "Zechariah 9," 37–59. Roberts, "Contribution," 44, dates it to the Assyrian period on the basis of the places mentioned.

32. J. J. Collins, "Eschatology," 74–84.

33. Horbury, *Jewish Messianism*, 68–77.

34. J. J. Collins, "Messianism and Exegetical Tradition," 58–81.

35. Munnich, "Messianisme."

36. For a maximalist view of messianism in the Greek Psalter, see Schaper, *Eschatology*, 72–126.

37. For the following, see J. J. Collins, *Scepter and the Star*. See also Charlesworth, Lichtenberger, and Oegema, *Qumran-Messianism*; Pomykala, *Davidic Dynasty*, 171–216; Zimmermann, *Messianische Texte*; Xeravits, *King, Priest, Prophet*.

38. J. J. Collins, *Scepter and the Star*, 49–73.

39. Atkinson, *I Cried to the Lord*, especially pp. 129–79 on the messianism of the Psalms in light of the Dead Sea Scrolls.

40. J. J. Collins, *Scepter and the Star*, 74–101.

41. Puech, "4QApocryphe," 165–84.

42. This was originally suggested by J. T. Milik in a lecture at Harvard in December, 1972. Vermes, *Complete Dead Sea Scrolls*, 617, decides to sit on the fence and apply the title either to a Davidic messiah or a historical Seleucid pretender. So also Puech. The fullest defence of the negative interpretation is that of Cook, "4Q246," 43–66.

43. To the best of my knowledge, the messianic interpretation was first proposed orally by F. M. Cross. See his discussion in *Ancient Library of Qumran*, 189–91. So also J. J. Collins, "Son of God Text from Qumran," 65–82; idem, *Scepter and the Star*, 154–72; Xeravits, *King, Priest, Prophet*, 88–89; Zimmermann, *Messianische Texte*, 162 (Xeravits speaks of a positive eschatological figure with Davidic associations rather than of a messiah). Fitzmyer, "4Q246," 41–61, also sees the figure as positive, a Jewish king in an apocalyptic context, but insists that he is not messianic.

44. See further J. J. Collins, "Herald of Good Tidings," 225–40.

45. Puech, "Fragments d'un apocryphe," 2.449–501; Starcky, "Quatres étapes," 481–505 (492).

46. J. J. Collins, *Scepter and the Star*, 123–26.

47. Wise, *First Messiah*, 92, 290.

48. J. J. Collins, *Daniel*, 304–10.

49. Koch, "Messias und Menschensohn," 235–66; Müller, *Messias und Menschensohn*.

50. See further J. J. Collins, *Apocalyptic Imagination*, 117–93.

51. Kobelski, *Melchizedek and Melchireša*, 49–74.

52. Stone, *Fourth Ezra*.

53. In light of this, it is unlikely that the underlying Hebrew had

"servant" rather than "son" as suggested by Stone, *Fourth Ezra*, 207–13 ("Excursus on the Redeemer Figure").
  54. Schaper, *Eschatology*, 102.
  55. J. J. Collins, "Sibylline Oracles," 390–405.
  56. Horbury, "Messianic Associations," 150.
  57. On these figures, see especially Horsley and Hanson, *Bandits, Prophets, and Messiahs*, esp. 88–134; J. J. Collins, *Scepter and the Star*, 195–214.
  58. See now Rajak, "Jewish Millenarian Expectations," 164–88.
  59. Hengel, "Messianische Hoffnung," 653–84. On this revolt, see now Pucci Ben Zeev, *Diaspora Judaism in Turmoil*.
  60. *y. Taʿan.* 4:8. For a critical treatment of the sources see Schäfer, *Bar Kokhba Aufstand*; idem, "Aqiva and Bar Kokhba," 113–30.
  61. Neusner, *Messiah in Context*.
  62. Levey, *Messiah*.
  63. On messianic expectation in rabbinic literature and the Targums, see now Fitzmyer, *The One Who is to Come*, 146–81.

2. The Messiah as Son of God in the Synoptic Gospels

  1. A. Y. Collins, "Establishing the Text," 111–27; Ehrman, "Text of Mark," 19–31; idem, *Orthodox Corruption*, 72–75; Head, "Text-Critical Study," 621–29.
  2. The verb *eudokēsa* in v. 11 is an ingressive aorist; see Smyth, *Greek Grammar*, § 1924. All translations are by the author unless otherwise indicated.
  3. On the equivalence of "Messiah" and "Son of Man" in the first century CE, see A. Y. Collins, "Influence of Daniel," 90–112, esp. 90–105.
  4. E.g., see Liebers, *"Wie geschrieben steht,"* 369–76.
  5. A. Y. Collins, "Mark and His Readers," 85–100; Moss, "Transfiguration," 69–89.
  6. A. Y. Collins, "Son of God," 86–87.
  7. On Elijah, see Josephus, *A.J* 9.28. On Moses, see Josephus, *A.J* 4.325–326. In spite of the statement in Deut 34:5 that Moses died, Josephus did not believe that he did; see Begg, "Josephus' Portrayal," 691–93, esp. 692; see also A. Y. Collins, *Beginning of the Gospel*, 142–43.
  8. Cf. 1 Sam 10:1; 1 Kgs 19:15–16.
  9. Cf. Mark 8:30–31.
  10. On the ambiguity of the centurion's statement, see A. Y.

Collins, "Son of God," 93–97. See also Shiner, "Ambiguous Pronouncement," 3–22.

11. The transformation of the earthly Jesus as Messiah-designate into the exalted, heavenly Messiah explains why the Markan Jesus questions the idea of the Messiah as the son of David (Mark 12:35–37; cf. Matt 22:41–46).

12. The preposition *ek* here is apparently used as a marker denoting origin or cause; see BAG, *s.v.* 3.

13. Cf. Luz, *Matthew 1–7*, 120.

14. Davies and Allison, *Matthew 1–7*, 214. So also Brown, *Birth of the Messiah*, 149.

15. Brown, *Birth of the Messiah*, 149. So also Davies and Allison, *Matthew 1–7*, 214.

16. Davies and Allison discuss proposals regarding "an historical catalyst," but find these theories problematic (*Matthew 1–7*, 216).

17. See the list given in Davies and Allison, *Matthew 1–7*, 214. See also Cartlidge and Dungan, *Documents*, 129–36.

18. Plutarch *Num.* 4.4; for a text and translation, see Perrin (LCL). Davies and Allison refer to this passage (*Matthew 1–7*, 201). See also the discussion in Bovon, *Luke 1*, 43–47, esp. 46 and n. 27.

19. Brown concluded that Matt 1:18–25 portrays Jesus as God's son (*Birth of the Messiah*, 161); so also Luz, *Matthew 1–7*, 121. Davies and Allison, however, argued that others had "exaggerated the importance in 1.18–25 of Matthew's Son of God Christology" (*Matthew 1–7*, 201, n. 9). This perspective leads them to disregard the notion of Jesus as son of God in their interpretation of the name "Emmanuel" (see p. 217).

20. At the end of Matt 1:23.

21. See the criticisms of this view in Davies and Allison, *Matthew 1–7*, 217.

22. By ignoring the implication that Jesus is Son of God here, Davies and Allison (*Matthew 1–7*, 217) seem to imply this kind of interpretation.

23. The subordination of the son to the Father seems to be implied in Mark 13:32 and its parallel in Matt 24:36; cf. 1 Cor 15:27–28.

24. 2 Sam 7:13–14, 15; Brown, *Birth of the Messiah*, 310 (emphasis his). So also Bovon, *Luke 1*, 51.

25. Dan 7:14; translation from J. J. Collins, *Daniel*, 275. Fitzmyer (*Luke I–IX*, 348) concludes that Luke may allude here to Isa 9:6 LXX or to Dan 7:14.

26. On the translation of the last clause, see Brown, *Birth of the Messiah*, 286; Fitzmyer, *Luke I–IX*, 334, 351; Bovon, *Luke 1*, 43, 52.

27. In his discussion of the context of this narrative in the history of religion, Bovon emphasizes Egyptian religion and pharaonic ideology (*Luke 1*, 43–47, esp. 46). See, however, his references to Plutarch and Philo.

3. Paul and the Missing Messiah

1. I would like to thank Samuel Byrskog and Bengt Holmberg for their helpful comments on an earlier version of this article.
2. On the relation between *story* and *history* in the Gospels, see Byrskog, *Story*, 1–6, 297–99.
3. Scripture quotations are from the NRSV.
4. Matt 26:26–29; Mark 14:22–25; Luke 22:14–20. Cf. also Rom 12:1–15:13; 1 Cor 7:10, 9:14; 1 Thess 4:1–12, 4:13–5:11, which may reveal that Paul was aware of the teachings of Jesus; see Longenecker, "Christological Material," 62–63. See also the discussion in Dunn, *Theology*, 185–95, and Kim, *Paul*, 259–90.
5. Kramer, *Christ*, 162.
6. Dunn, *Theology*, 208–9.
7. Eriksson, *Traditions*, 74–76. See also Rom 6:17; Gal 1:9; Phil 4:9; Col 2:6; 1 Thess 2:13; 2 Thess 3:6.
8. For an overview of the concept of *māšîaḥ* and the practice of anointing, see Talmon, "Concept," 79–115. On the anointing of the king, see Mettinger, *King and Messiah*, 185–232, and on the legal function of anointing, see Viberg, *Symbols*, 89–119.
9. On different popular messianic movements around the time of Jesus, see Horsley, "Messianic Movements," 471–95; Horsley and Hanson, *Bandits, Prophets, and Messiahs*.
10. The words "Son of God" are missing from some important manuscripts, and it is likely that they were not part of the original wording but were added later by a copyist; see the discussion in A. Y. Collins, "Establishing the Text," 111–25.
11. Hooker, *Mark*, 34.
12. Dunn, *Christology in the Making*, 46–47.
13. See also Mark 1:9–11, 3:11, 5:7.
14. Cf. Matt 26:63–64; Luke 22:67–70.
15. Hooker, "Who Can This Be?" 81–82; A. Y. Collins, "Influence," 97–98.
16. Juel, *Messianic Exegesis*, 13.
17. Juel, "Origin," 449–60.
18. While John usually uses the Greek translation *christos* for

"Messiah," he actually transcribes the word twice; see John 1:41 (acc.), 4:25 (nom.).

19. For an overview, see Ladd, *Theology*, 159–72.

20. Hurtado, "Paul's Christology," 191; Kramer, *Christ*, 189; Moo, "Christology," 187–88.

21. See, e.g., Dunn, *Theology*, 197; Fredriksen, *From Jesus to Christ*, 56; Hengel, "Christological Titles," 444; Hurtado, "Paul's Christology," 191; Kramer, *Christ*, 67–68, 203–14; Kümmel, *Theology*, 154; Moo, "Christology," 186.

22. Hengel, *Between Jesus and Paul*, 67. For a short overview of Paul's use of *christos* compared to the use in the rest of the NT, see Shiner and Aune, "Christian Prophecy," 405–6.

23. Hengel, *Between Jesus and Paul*, 67.

24. Dunn, *Theology*, 244–45; Hengel, "Christological Titles," 441–42; Kümmel, *Theology*, 157; Moo, "Christology," 188. On Paul's use of *kyrios*, see also Kramer, *Christ*, 151–82.

25. Kramer, *Christ*, 21.

26. Ibid., 34–35.

27. Ibid., 23–24, 44.

28. Ibid., 24–25.

29. א C D a b sy bo 𝔐.

30. Kramer precludes an origin within the Aramaic-speaking part of the early Jesus movement (see Kramer, *Christ*, 69–71, 83). Hengel, on the other hand, suggests that early interpretations of Ps 110:1 encouraged and introduced the use of "Lord" within the earliest Palestinian communities, which can be seen in the acclamation of the Aramaic *Maranatha*, "our Lord come!" (cf. Rev 22:20; 1 Cor 16:22); see Hengel, "Christological Titles," 438–39. So also Fitzmyer, *Wandering Aramean*, 123–30.

31. Kramer, *Christ*, 80–84.

32. Ibid., 182.

33. Ibid., 182.

34. Gaston, *Paul and the Torah*, 115; Hengel, "Christological Titles," 442.

35. Hengel, "Christological Titles," 440.

36. See, e.g., Rom 9:5.

37. Dahl, "Messiahship," 38.

38. See, e.g., Bultmann, *Primitive Christianity*, 176–77; Fuller, *Foundations*, 86–87; Kramer, *Christ*, 212–13; Ladd, *Theology*, 417; Vermes, *Changing Faces*, 84.

39. Transl. by Thackeray (LCL).

40. Cohen, "Respect," 417.

41. Feldman, *Jew and Gentile*, 350; Goodman, *Mission and Conversion*, 87.
42. Harland, *Associations*, 115–36; Zetterholm, *Formation of Christianity*, 25–28.
43. Transl. by Green (LCL).
44. Transl. by Lauterbach (*Mekilta de R. Yismael*).
45. Hirshman, "Rabbinic Universalism," 103.
46. Ibid., 107–8.
47. Ibid., 112.
48. Transl. by Colson (LCL).
49. Stowers, *Rereading Romans*, 58. Similar statements also can be found in Josephus, especially in *Contra Apionem*; see Cohen, "Respect," 409–30. See also Stowers's entire discussion of Judaism and self-mastery in *Rereading Romans*, 58–74. On *didaskaleion* as a term for designating a synagogue, see also Binder, *Temple Courts*, 133–35; Levine, *Ancient Synagogue*, 82–83; Runesson, *Origins*, 171–72.
50. Nock, *Conversion*, 7.
51. Beard, et al., *Religions of Rome*, 245.
52. See, e.g., Price, *Religions*, 3–10, on the Panhellenic religious system and Harland, *Associations*, 115–36, for the somewhat broader imperial context.
53. See, e.g., McGuire, *Religion*, 72–73; Rambo, *Religious Conversion*, 12–14.
54. Stark, *Rise of Christianity*, 18. See also Stark's references to other studies, which all give ample evidence of the importance of social networks and personal attachments in connection with conversion.
55. Ibid., 16–17.
56. Ibid., 18.
57. Ibid., 55. See also Stark, *Cities of God*, 126–29, for this general sociological principle.
58. *Contra* Slee, *Church in Antioch*, 24.
59. See Gager, *Reinventing Paul*, 21–42, for an overview of the traditional view of Paul.
60. On Christian views of Judaism, see e.g., Moore, "Christian Writers," 197–254; Sanders, *Palestinian Judaism*, 33–59.
61. Ibid., 419–28.
62. See, e.g., Gaston, *Paul and the Torah*; Nanos, *Mystery*; idem, *Irony*; Stendahl, *Paul*; idem, *Final Account*; Stowers, *Rereading Romans*. See also the overview in Gager, *Reinventing Paul*, 43–75.
63. Cited from Fraade, *Tradition to Commentary*, 57.
64. Ibid., 57–58.
65. Transl. by Abramowitz (*The Mishnah: A New Translation with a Commentary by Rabbi Pinhas Kehati*).

66. On this text, see also Hirshman, "Rabbinic Universalism," 105–6.

67. Nanos, *Mystery*, 184.

68. See, e.g., Isa 2:2–3, 19:18–25; *1 En.* 10:21, 90:30–33, 91:14; *Sib. Or.* 3:564–570; Tob 13:11. See also the discussion in Zetterholm, *Formation of Christianity*, 136–40.

69. Sanders, *Palestinian Judaism*, 147–50, 422.

70. On the Jewish background to Jesus' lordship, see now Wright, "Paul's Gospel," 168–70.

71. Ibid., 168.

72. See, e.g., Dio Cassius 67.14.1–2; Suetonius, *Dom.* 15.1. On Roman control of the religious landscape, see Beard, et al., *Religions of Rome*, 228–44, 339–48.

73. Crossan and Reed, *In Search of Paul*, 250.

74. Brunt, *"Laus Imperii,"* 25–26; Burkert, *Greek Religion*, 64–68, 72–75, 254–60; Turcan, *Ancient Rome*, 5–6.

75. On the religious reforms under Augustus, see Beard, et al., *Religions of Rome*, 182–210.

76. Ibid., 206–9.

77. Crossan and Reed, *In Search of Paul*, 241. On the imperial cult, see also Price, "Rituals and Power," 47–71.

78. Tellbe, *Synagogue and State*, 35–51.

79. See Zetterholm, "Purity and Anger," 11–16.

80. On the political implications of Paul's gospel, see now Elliott, *Liberating Paul*; idem, "Anti-Imperial Message," 167–83.

81. The Antioch incident (Gal 2:11–14) is commonly thought to have involved a conflict between Torah observance (mainly ritual purity laws and food laws) and faith in Jesus among Jewish believers in Jesus (see e.g., Bornkamm, *Paul*, 45–46; Das, *Paul*, 156; Dunn, "Incident," 3–57; Holmberg, "Christian Identity," 397–425; Sanders, "Jewish Associations," 170–88), but it is more likely that the conflict concerned the *status* of non-Jewish believers in Jesus; see Nanos, "Peter's Eating," 282–318; Zetterholm, *Formation of Christianity*, 129–64; idem, "Purity and Anger," 16–20.

82. Stowers, *Rereading Romans*, 310.

4. Elijah and the Messiah as Spokesmen of Rabbinic Ideology

1. I would like to thank Mira Balberg for her helpful comments on an earlier draft of this article.

2. Milikowsky, "Trajectories," 265; Neusner, *Messiah in Context*, xi.

3. E.g., Joseph Klausner's *The Messianic Idea in Israel* (1956) and Gershom Scholem's *The Messianic Idea in Judaism* (1971).

4. Alexander, "King Messiah," 469.

5. Neusner, *Messiah in Context*, ix, 25–30, 229.

6. Alexander, "King Messiah," 471–73; Neusner, *Messiah in Context*, 167–231.

7. Horsley, "Popular Messianic Movements"; Horsley and Hanson, *Bandits, Prophets, and Messiahs*.

8. See e.g., Horbury (*Jewish Messianism*, 79) who, despite the near-silence of the Mishnah on the subject of the Messiah, emphasizes the importance of messianism within the Jewish community as testified by prayers, such as the *"Amidah"* by the Targums, and by the uprisings in the Diaspora under Trajan and the Bar Kokhba revolt in Judaea under Hadrian. See also Neusner (*Messiah in Context*, 226), who points out that the first and second centuries "encompassed the greatest messianic explosion in the history of Judaism."

9. Horsley, "Popular Messianic Movements," 471–75, 480; Horsley and Hanson, *Bandits, Prophets, and Messiahs*, xiii–xvi, 161.

10. Horsley, "'Prophets of Old,'" 443–45, 456, 460, 462.

11. Schwartz, *Imperialism*, 49–87.

12. Alexander, "King Messiah," 470; Neusner, *Messiah in Context*, 226.

13. Neusner, *Messiah in Context*, 31–42, 231. See also Lapin, "Hegemony," 341–42, who suggested that the Mishnah's disregard of world events; the choice to describe a utopian world in which the Roman presence in Palestine is rarely referred to and in which the temple still stands and forms the focus of much of the legal discussions; and the interpretation of world events within the frame of local concerns and interests are strategies utilized for the purpose of articulating a Jewish identity. Yerushalmi (*Zakhor*, 16–26) advances the idea that the lack of interest in recording historical events in rabbinic literature generally is due to the rabbis' complete absorption of the biblical interpretation of history in such a way that they considered new interpretations unnecessary.

14. Translations of biblical passages are from the new *Jewish Publication Society* translation, but when appearing in Talmudic passages, the quotes are sometimes modified to make the Talmudic exegesis comprehensible. Translations of Mishnah texts are based upon P. Kehati's *The Mishnah*. In translating passages from the Jerusalem and Babylonian Talmuds, I consulted J. Neusner's *The Talmud of the Land of Israel* and the Steinsaltz edition of the Babylonian Talmud.

15. Ben Sira (ca 180 BCE) expands this statement to mean that Elijah also will restore the tribes of Jacob to their homeland (48:10).

16. *Lev. Rab.* 34.8. In *S. ʿOlam Rab.* ch. 17, this duty is assigned to Elijah alone.

17. *m. B. Meṣiʿa* 1:8, 2:8, 3:4–5; *m. Šeqal.* 2:5.

18. Eisenberg, *JPS Guide*, 289–90; Schauss, *Jewish Festivals*, 80–1.

19. *b. ʿErub.* 43a–b; *Pesiq. Rab.* 35.3, *Pirqe R. El.* ch. 43; and *Tg. Ps.-J.* to Deut 30:4.

20. See Faierstein, "Scribes," 75–77, and the references cited there.

21. Ibid., 75–86; Fitzmyer, "Elijah Coming First," 295–96.

22. Milikowsky, "Trajectories," 268–77.

23. Horsley, "'Prophets of Old,'" 439, 443.

24. Neusner, *Messiah in Context*, 29–30.

25. *Sipre* pisqa 34; *Gen. Rab.* 74.1; *y. Kil.* 9:4 (9:3), *y. Ketub.* 12:3. See also Milikowsky, 269 n. 12. According to Puech's restoration, it is probable that the MS B Hebrew text of Sir 48:11 attests to the belief that Elijah will be the agent of the resurrection of the dead; see Xeravits, *King, Priest, Prophet*, 186.

26. *m. B. Meṣiʿa* 1:8, 2:8, 3:4–5; *m. Šeqal.* 2:5.

27. Hedner-Zetterholm, "Elijah's Roles."

28. Gafni, "Josephus," 118–19; idem, "Concepts," 32; Gray, *Prophetic Figures*, 7–34.

29. *t. Soṭah* 13:3; *y. Soṭah* 9:14; *b. Soṭah* 48b; *b. Yoma* 9b; *b. B. Bat.* 14b; *S. ʿOlam Rab.* ch. 30.

30. Bokser, "Wonder-Working," 78–81; Daube, "Enfant Terrible," 372; Freyne, *Ideal Figures*, 232; Green, "Palestinian Holy Men," 625–26; Vermes, "Hanina II," 62–64; idem, *Jesus the Jew*, 80–82.

31. See, Alexander, "King Messiah," 467, n. 22. Although he himself does not doubt the Tannaitic provenance of the *baraita*, "It was taught in the School of Eliahu . . . ," at *b. Sanh.* 97a, Urbach, *Sages*, 678 and n. 95, points out that it has no parallels in the Jerusalem Talmud or in the classical midrashim, a fact that is considered good reason for suspecting that such *baraitot* contain material from post-tannaitic times. See Friedman, "Literary Dependencies," 43–57; Rubenstein, *Culture*, 8.

32. Neusner, *Messiah in Context*, 169–75; Urbach, *Sages*, 677–683.

33. The first dispute between Rabbi Eliezer and Rabbi Yehoshua gives the impression that they both agree that repentance is a necessary prerequisite for redemption; Rabbi Yehoshua arguing that if [the people] Israel do not repent of their own will, God will make them repent by appointing a king as cruel as Haman over them. However, in the parallel passage in the Jerusalem Talmud (*y. Taʿan.* 1:1), the idea that God will make Israel repent is attributed to Rabbi Eliezer suggesting that the statement attributed to Rabbi Yehoshua in the Babylonian Talmud was originally two statements. One was by Rabbi

Yehoshua, followed by a response by Rabbi Eliezer, claiming that Israel will be made to repent. If read this way, we have a dispute where Rabbi Eliezer claims that redemption is a necessary prerequisite for redemption, while Rabbi Yehoshua maintains that Israel will be redeemed even without redemption, consistent with the dispute that follows between the same two rabbis.

34. Urbach, *Sages*, 683.

35. Fifty-year periods.

36. *m. B. Meṣiʿa* 1:8, 2:8, 3:4–5; *m. Šeqal.* 2:5; *m. ʿEd.* 8:7.

37. See e.g., *b. B. Meṣiʿa* 59b; *b. Ḥag.* 15b; *b. Giṭ.* 6b.

38. See Lindbeck, *Story and Theology*, 290–91; Urbach, *Sages*, 680.

39. Rubenstein, *Talmudic Stories*, 54 and n. 67.

40. Lindbeck, *Story and Theology*, 305–7. For an analysis of the first part of the story, the meeting between Elijah and Rabbi Yehoshua ben Levi taking place at the entrance of Rabbi Shimon ben Yohai's burial cave, Rabbi Yehoshua ben Levi's question about entering the world to come and the voices he heard, and the possibility that these components derive from another source where they made better sense, see idem, *Story and Theology*, 308–11.

41. The Hebrew of the quotation from Isa 21:11 is *ʾēlay qōrēʾ miśśēʿîr* and in its context, it means "someone calls to me from Seir," but *ʿ-l-y* can mean either "to me" or "my God." Seir, the land of the Edomites, descendants of Esau, is identified with Rome in many rabbinic texts. For the origin of the identification of Esau and Seir and Rome, see Cohen, "Esau as Symbol," 19–48.

42. For the techniques of the Bavli redactors in reworking Palestinian stories, see Friedman, "Literary Development," 70–71; Rubenstein, *Talmudic Stories*, 244; idem, "Stammaitic Intervention."

43. Fraenkel points out that this description of the Messiah is borrowed in part from Isa 53:4, quoted in Lindbeck, *Story and Theology*, 313; and Alexander, "King Messiah," 463, remarks that this description of the Messiah has a Christian coloring.

44. Rav Nahman asks Rabbi Yitzhak, and the latter answers that the Messiah will come at a time when Torah scholars will be few in number and sorrow and disaster great (*b. Sanh.* 96b–97a). Rabbi Yose ben Kisma is asked by his disciples and reluctantly answers that the Messiah will come when "this gate has fallen" and been rebuilt twice, then fallen yet a third time (*b. Sanh.* 98a). A *min* asks Rabbi Abbahu, who says that the Messiah will come "when darkness covers those people" (*b. Sanh.* 99a). See Lindbeck, *Story and Theology*, 311–12. In addition to the question asked twice in our passage by Rabbi Yehoshua ben Levi, once to Elijah and once to the Messiah himself,

Rav Yehudah, the brother of Rav Salla, also poses the question to Elijah in the passage discussed previously (*b. Sanh.* 97b).

45. The idea that it is Israel's conduct that prevents the Messiah from coming also is expressed in another discussion between Elijah and Rav Yehudah, brother of Rav Salla the Pious: Elijah said to Rav Yehudah, brother of Rav Salla the Pious, "You have asked, 'Why has the Messiah not come?' Now, today is the Day of Atonement, and yet how many virgins were embraced in Nehardea?" (*b. Yoma* 19b).

46. Lindbeck, *Story and Theology*, 289–90.

47. See, Boyarin, *Border Lines*, 143. The expression *maḥyûhû šitîn pûlsēy děnûrā*ʾ seems to be a characteristic of the Babylonian Talmud and appears outside it only in late midrashim, which may be dependant on it; see Halperin, *Merkabah*, 169–70 and n. 100.

48. Lindbeck, *Story and Theology*, 297. The story in *b. Ḥag.* 15a also appears to support human freedom by subtly protesting the Mishnah's opposition to esoteric study (*m. Ḥag.* 2:1); see Rubenstein, *Talmudic Stories*, 101. Further similarities between the two stories concern Elijah and Metatron who share certain traits apart from their common punishment. Metatron is said to record the merits of Israel; and Elijah is elsewhere, as noted, said to record man's good deeds (*Lev. Rab.* 34.8; *S. ʿOlam Rab.* ch. 17). Furthermore, they can both be said to tempt the human protagonists; Metatron by behaving in a way that led Elisha to believe that there was more than one divine power in heaven and Elijah by revealing heavenly knowledge that caused the rabbis to engage in forbidden activities.

49. Lindbeck, *Story and Theology*, 299.

50. Ibid., 303–4.

51. As previously mentioned, charismatic figures such as Honi the Circle-Drawer and Hanina ben Dosa, who claimed access to God through magical means, evoked mixed feelings among the rabbis; see e.g., Daube, "Enfant Terrible"; Freyne, "Ideal Figures"; Green, "Palestinian Holy Men."

52. Lindbeck, *Story and Theology*, 307.

53. Neusner, *Messiah in Context*, 184–85.

54. Ibid., 176–77, 186.

55. As Lindbeck, *Story and Theology*, 303–4, points out, this is not to imply that such stories were written with the sole purpose of reinforcing rabbinic authority, but the issue of authority may nevertheless have played a role in the rabbinization of the Messiah.

56. Boyarin, "Tale," 47.

57. Neusner, *Messiah in Context*, 230–31.

58. Hedner-Zetterholm, "Elijah's Roles."

59. It should be stated clearly that I do not imply that the rabbis were deliberately manipulating the people and trying to enforce their power and authority. Rather, I believe that they were trying to convince themselves as much as others of the legitimacy of their authority.

5. The Reception of Messianism and the Worship of Christ in the Post-Apostolic Church

1. Pliny the Younger, *Ep.* 10.96; Tacitus, *Ann.* 15.44; Suetonius, *Nero* 16. For discussion, see Wilken, *Christians*, 48–50.
2. Minucius Felix, *Oct.* 9; Theophilus of Antioch, *Autol.* 3.4.
3. Hargis, *Against the Christians*, 12–14. The Christian apologist Athenagoras of Athens attests in his *Legatio pro Christianis*, composed about 177 CE, that the main charges against Christians at this time were three in number: atheism, Thyestean banquets (cannibalism), and Oedipodal unions (incest). See *Leg.* 3.1.
4. Wilken, *Christians*, 92.
5. Transl. by Cary and Foster (LCL).
6. Wilken, *Christians*, 62–63.
7. Transl. by Thelwall (*ANF*).
8. Tertullian, *Apol.* 19.2.
9. Tertullian, *Apol.* 20.
10. Tertullian, *Apol.* 21.6.
11. Tertullian, *Apol.* 21.5.
12. See Lieu, *Neither Jew Nor Greek?*, 121–26.
13. Transl. by Roberts and Donaldson (*ANF*).
14. Lieu, *Image*, 111–12.
15. Justin, *Dial.* 9.1.
16. Justin, *Dial.* 32.1.
17. Justin, *Dial.* 38.1.
18. Justin, *Dial.* 56.
19. Justin, *Dial.* 75.1–3.
20. Justin, *Dial.* 32.6–33.3; 56.14.
21. Justin, *Dial.* 56.14.
22. Beskow, *Rex Gloriae*, 85.
23. Justin, *Dial.* 11.5.
24. Justin, *Dial.* 16.4; 35.7–8; 47.4; 93.4; 95.4; 96.2; 108.3; 122.2; 133.6.
25. Hargis, *Against the Christians*, 37–38.
26. Transl. by Crombie (*ANF*).
27. Origen, *Cels.* 2.1.

28. Cf. Origen, *Cels.* 2.4.
29. Beskow, *Rex Gloriae,* 219–27.
30. Transl. by Beskow (*Rex Gloriae*).
31. See King, *Origen.*
32. Jerome, *Comm. Isa.*, prol. 18; Newman, "Jerome's Judaizers," 436–44.
33. For a comprehensive historical survey of chiliasm, see Baumgartner, *Longing for the End.*
34. Cf. Daley, *Hope,* 17–18.
35. Lieu, *Image,* 5–6.
36. See Daley, *Hope,* 18.
37. See Frankfurter, "Legacy," 132–33.
38. A. Y. Collins, *Crisis,* 46–48.
39. Hill, *Regnum Caelorum,* 41–44; Aune, "Apocalypse of John."
40. Transl. by Metzger (*OTP*).
41. See Horbury, *Messianism,* 63–64.
42. Transl. by Klijn (*OTP*).
43. See J. J. Collins, *Apocalyptic Imagination,* 210–14; Bauckham, *Climax,* 38–91.
44. Hill, *Regnum Caelorum,* 57–63.
45. Transl. by Roberts and Donaldson (*ANF*).
46. Transl. by McGiffert (*NPNF²*).
47. Eusebius, *Hist. eccl.* 3:39.2–7.
48. For discussion, see Hill, "Papias of Hierapolis," 309–10.
49. Ibid., 313–14.
50. Eusbeius, *Hist. eccl.* 7.25.1–2.
51. Harnack, "Millennium," 316.
52. Hill, "Cerinthus," 135–72.
53. Tertullian, *Marc.* 4.6.
54. Tertullian, *Marc.* 3.24.
55. See Hill, "Antichrist," 99–117.
56. Idem, "Cerinthus," 162–63.
57. Irenaeus, *Haer.* 1.26.1
58. Irenaeus, *Haer.* 3.12.2. Hill admits the lack of any mention of Cerinthus in this passage but concludes that the text must refer to Cerinthus through the adoptionist tendency of the opinions attacked by Irenaeus (cf. *Haer.* 1.26.1). Hill rules out that the passage could refer to Marcian, as there is no adoptionist doctrine in Marcian's Christology, or to the Valentinians, who believed that Jesus was predicted by the Old Testament prophets; see Hill, "Cerinthus," 163 and n. 76.
59. Hill, "Cerinthus,"163–64.

60. Ibid., 164–67.
61. Transl. by Amidon (*Panarion*).
62. Hill, "Marriage of Montanism," 142. Trevett, *Montanism*, 96.
63. Trevett, *Montanism*, 96.
64. Eusebius, *Hist. eccl.* 5.18.2.
65. Powell, "Tertullianists and Cataphrygians," 44–46; Trevett, *Montanism*, 99–105. For a critical discussion about the often-assumed role of Montanism in the chiliasm of Tertullian, see Hill, "Marriage of Montanism," 142–48.
66. Wilken, "Early Christian Chiliasm," 305.
67. Transl. by Roberts and Donaldson (*ANF*).
68. Hill, *Regnum Caelorum*, 23.
69. Cf. *Dial.* 139.
70. For instance, Daley, *Hope*, 20–22.
71. Hill, *Regnum Caelorum*, 20.
72. Justin, *Dial.* 80.
73. Hill, *Regnum Caelorum*, 9–13.
74. Smith, "Chiliasm," 313–15.
75. Irenaeus, *Haer.* 5.28.3. Smith, "Chiliasm," 315–18.
76. Smith, "Chiliasm," 318–19.
77. Irenaeus, *Haer.* 5.36.1–2.
78. Irenaeus, *Haer.* 5.35.2; 5.36.1. Smith, "Chiliasm," 319.
79. Irenaeus, *Haer.* 5.36.2.
80. Smith, "Chiliasm," 126–29.
81. Origen, *Cels.* 7.28. Plato, *Phaed.* 109A, B.
82. Transl. by Crombie (*ANF*).
83. Wilken, "Early Christian Chiliasm," 307. Cf. Origen, *Princ.* 4.2.1.

BIBLIOGRAPHY

Alexander, P. S. "The King Messiah in Rabbinic Judaism." In *King and Messiah in Israel and the Ancient Near East: Proceedings of the Oxford Old Testament Seminar*, edited by J. Day. JSOTSup 270. Sheffield: Sheffield Academic, 1998.

Alt, A. "Jesaja 8,23–9,6. Befreiungsmacht und Krönungstag." In *Festschrift Alfred Bertholet zum 80. Geburtstag gewidmet*, edited by W. Baumgartner. Tübingen: Mohr Siebeck, 1950.

Amidon, P. R. *The Panarion of St. Epiphanius, Bishop of Salamis: Selected Passages*. New York: Oxford University Press, 1990.

Ante-Nicene Fathers. Edited by A. Roberts and J. Donaldson. 1885–1887. 10 vols. Repr. Peabody: Hendrickson, 1994.

Assmann, J. "Die Zeugung des Sohnes: Bild, Spiel, Erzählung und das Problem des ägyptischen Mythos." In J. Assman, W. Burkert, and F. Stoltz, *Funktionen und Leistungen des Mythos: Drei altorientalische Beispiele*. OBO 48. Freiburg: Universitätsverlag, 1982.

Atkinson, K. *"I Cried to the Lord": A Study of the Psalms of Solomon's Historical Background and Social Setting*. Supplements to the *Journal for the Study of Judaism* 84. Leiden: Brill, 2004.

Augustine. *The City of God Against the Pagans*. Translated by W. M. Green et al. 7 vols. Loeb Classical Library. Cambridge: Harvard University Press, 1957–.

Aune, D. E. "The Apocalypse of John and the Palestinian Jewish Apocalyptic." *Neot* 40 (2006): 1–33.

Bauckham, R. *The Climax of Prophecy: Studies on the Book of Revelation*. Edinburgh: T&T Clark, 1993.

Bauer, W., W. F. Arndt, F. W. Danker, and F. W. Gingrich. *A Greek-English Lexicon of the New Testament and Other Early Christian Literature.* 3rd ed. Chicago: University of Chicago Press, 2000.

Baumgartner, F. J. *Longing for the End: A History of Millennialism in Western Civilization.* New York: Palgrave, 2001.

Beard, M. et al. *Religions of Rome: Volume One: A History.* Cambridge: Cambridge University Press, 1998.

Begg, C. T. "Josephus's Portrayal of the Disappearances of Enoch, Elijah and Moses: Some Observations." *JBL* 109 (1990): 691–93.

Beskow, P. *Rex Gloriae: The Kingship of Christ in the Early Church.* Stockholm: Almqvist & Wiksell, 1962.

Binder, D. D. *Into the Temple Courts: The Place of the Synagogue in the Second Temple Period.* SBLDS 169. Atlanta: Society of Biblical Literature, 1999.

Blenkinsopp, J. *A History of Prophecy in Israel.* 2nd ed. Louisville: Westminster John Knox, 1996.

———. *Isaiah 1–39: A New Translation with Introduction and Commentary.* AB 19. New York: Doubleday, 2000.

Bokser, B. M. "Wonder-Working and the Rabbinic Tradition: The Case of Hanina Ben Dosa." *JSJ* 16 (1985): 42–92.

Bornkamm, G. *Paul.* Minneapolis: Fortress Press, 1995 [1969 in German].

Bovon, F. *Luke 1: A Commentary on the Gospel of Luke 1:1–9:50.* Hermeneia, edited by H. Koester. Minneapolis: Fortress Press, 2002.

Boyarin, D. *Border Lines: The Partition of Judaeo-Christianity.* Philadelphia: University of Pennsylvania Press, 2004.

———. "A Tale of Two Synods: Nicaea, Yavneh, and Rabbinic Ecclesiology." *Exemplaria* 12 (2000): 21–62.

Brown, R. E. *The Birth of the Messiah: A Commentary on the Infancy Narratives in the Gospels of Matthew and Luke.* New York: Doubleday, 1993 [1977].

Brunner, H. *Die Geburt des Gottkönigs: Studien zur Überlieferung eines altägyptischen Mythos.* Ägyptologische Abhandlungen 10. Wiesbaden: Harrassowitz, 1964.

Brunt, P. A. "Laus Imperii." In *Paul and Empire: Religion and Power in Roman Imperial Society*, edited by R. A. Horsley. Harrisburg: Trinity, 1997.

Bultmann, R. *Primitive Christianity in Its Contemporary Setting.* Cleveland: World, 1965.

Burkert, W. *Greek Religion.* Cambridge: Harvard University Press, 1985.

Byrskog, S. *Story as History—History as Story: The Gospel Tradition in the Context of Ancient Oral History*. WUNT 123. Tübingen: Mohr Siebeck, 2000.

Cartlidge, D. R. and D. L. Dungan. *Documents for the Study of the Gospels*. Philadelphia: Fortress Press, 1980.

Charlesworth, J. H., H. Lichtenberger, and G. S. Oegema, eds. *Qumran-Messianism: Studies on the Messianic Expectations in the Dead Sea Scrolls*. Tübingen: Mohr Siebeck, 1998.

Cohen, G. D. "Esau as Symbol in Early Medieval Thought." In *Jewish Medieval and Renaissance Studies*, edited by A. Altmann. P. W. Lown Institute of Advanced Judaic Studies. Cambridge: Harvard University Press, 1967.

Cohen, S. J. D. "Respect for Judaism by Gentiles According to Josephus." *HTR* 80 (1987): 409–30.

Collins, A. Y. *The Beginning of the Gospel: Probings of Mark in Context*. Minneapolis: Fortress Press, 1992.

———. *Crisis and Catharsis: The Power of the Apocalypse*. Philadelphia: Westminister, 1984.

———. "Establishing the Text: Mark 1:1." In *Texts and Contexts: The Function of Biblical Texts in Their Textual and Situational Contexts. Essays in Honor of Lars Hartman*, edited by T. Fornberg and D. Hellholm. Oslo: Scandinavian University Press, 1995.

———. "The Influence of Daniel on the New Testament." In J. J. Collins, *A Commentary on the Book of Daniel*. Hermeneia, edited by F. M. Cross. Minneapolis: Fortress Press, 1993.

———. "Mark and His Readers: The Son of God among Greeks and Romans." *HTR* 93 (2000): 85–100.

Collins, J. J. *The Apocalyptic Imagination: An Introduction to Jewish Apocalyptic Literature*. 2nd ed. Grand Rapids: Eerdmans, 1998.

———. *Daniel: A Commentary on the Book of Daniel*, edited by F. M. Cross. Hermeneia. Minneapolis: Fortress Press, 1993.

———. "The Eschatology of Zechariah." In *Knowing the End from the Beginning: The Prophetic, the Apocalyptic and their Relationships*. JSPSup 46, edited by L. L. Grabbe and R. D. Haak. London: Continuum, 2003.

———. "A Herald of Good Tidings: Isaiah 61:1–3 and its Actualization in the Dead Sea Scrolls." In *The Quest for Context and Meaning: Studies in Biblical Intertextuality in Honor of James A. Sanders*, edited by C. A. Evans and S. Talmon. Leiden: Brill, 1997.

———. "Messianism and Exegetical Tradition: The Evidence of the LXX Pentateuch." In *Jewish Cult and Hellenistic Culture: Essays on the Jewish Encounter with Hellenism and Roman Rule*. Supplements to the Journal for the Study of Judaism 100. Leiden: Brill, 2005.

————. *The Scepter and the Star: The Messiahs of the Dead Sea Scrolls and Other Ancient Literature*. ABRL. New York: Doubleday, 1995.

————. "The Sibylline Oracles." In *The Old Testament Pseudepigrapha: Volume 1: Apocalyptic Literature and Testaments*, edited by J. H. Charlesworth. New York: Doubleday, 1983.

————. "The 'Son of God' Text from Qumran." In *From Jesus to John: Essays on Jesus and New Testament Christology in Honour of Marinus de Jonge*. JSOT 84, edited by M. C. de Boer. Sheffield: JSOT Press, 1993.

Cook, E. M. "4Q246." *BBR* 5 (1995): 43–66.

Cross, F. M. *The Ancient Library of Qumran and Modern Biblical Studies*. 3rd ed. Sheffield: Sheffield Academic, 1995.

————. *Canaanite Myth and Hebrew Epic*. Cambridge: Harvard University Press, 1973.

Crossan, J. D. and J. L. Reed. *In Search of Paul: How Jesus's Apostle Opposed Rome's Empire with God's Kingdom: A New Vision of Paul's Words & World*. London: SPCK, 2005.

Dahl, N. A. "The Messiahship of Jesus in Paul." In N. A. Dahl, *The Crucified Messiah and Other Essays*. Minneapolis: Augsburg, 1974.

Daley, B. E. *The Hope of the Early Church: A Handbook of Patristic Eschatology*. Peabody: Hendrickson, 2003.

Dalley, S. *Myths from Mesopotamia*. Oxford: Oxford University Press, 1989.

Das, A. A. *Paul, the Law and the Covenant*. Peabody: Hendrickson, 2001.

Daube, D. "Enfant Terrible." *HTR* 68 (1975): 371–76.

Davies, W. D. and D. C. Allison. *A Critical and Exegetical Commentary on the Gospel According to Saint Matthew, Volume I, Matthew 1–7*. ICC, edited by J. A. Emerton, C. E. B. Cranfield, and G. N. Stanton. Edinburgh: T&T Clark, 2004 [1991].

Day, J. "The Canaanite Inheritance of the Israelite Monarchy." In *King and Messiah in Israel and the Ancient Near East*. JSOTSup 270, edited by J. Day. Sheffield: Sheffield Academic, 1998.

Dio Cassius. *Roman History*. Translated by E. Cary and H. B Foster. 9 vols. Loeb Classical Library. Cambridge: Harvard University Press, 1914–.

Duhm, B. *Das Buch Jesaja*. 4th ed. Göttingen: Vandenhoeck & Ruprecht, 1922 [1st ed. 1892].

Dunn, J. D. G. *Christology in the Making: An Inquiry into the Origins of the Doctrine of the Incarnation*. London: SCM Press, 1989.

————. "The Incident at Antioch (Gal. 2:11–18)." *JSNT* 18 (1983): 3–57.

————. *The Theology of Paul the Apostle*. London: T & T Clark, 2005 [1998].

Ehrman, B. *The Orthodox Corruption of Scripture: The Effect of Early Christological Controversies on the Text of the New Testament.* Oxford: Oxford University Press, 1996.

———. "The Text of Mark in the Hands of the Orthodox." In *Biblical Hermeneutics in Historical Perspective: Essays in Honor of Karlfried Froehlich,* edited by M. Burrows and P. Rorem. Grand Rapids: Eerdmans, 1991.

Eisenberg, R. L. *The JPS Guide to Jewish Traditions.* Philadelphia: Jewish Publication Society, 2004.

Elliott, N. "The Anti-Imperial Message of the Cross." In *Paul and Empire: Religion and Power in Roman Imperial Society,* edited by R. A. Horsley. Harrisburg: Trinity, 1997.

———. *Liberating Paul: The Justice of God and the Politics of the Apostle.* Sheffield: Sheffield Academic, 1995.

Eriksson, A. *Traditions as Rhetorical Proof: Pauline Argumentation in 1 Corinthians.* ConBNT 29. Stockholm: Almqvist & Wiksell, 1998.

Faierstein, M. "Why Do the Scribes Say That Elijah Must Come First?" *JBL* 100 (1981): 75–86.

Feldman, L. H. *Jew and Gentile in the Ancient World: Attitudes and Interactions from Alexander to Justinian.* Princeton: Princeton University Press, 1996.

Fishbane, M. *Biblical Interpretation in Ancient Israel.* Oxford: Clarendon, 1985.

Fitzmyer, J. A. *The Dead Sea Scrolls and Christian Origins. Studies in the Dead Sea Scrolls and Related Literature.* Grand Rapids: Eerdmans, 2000.

———. *The Gospel According to Luke: Introduction, Translation, and Notes,* Volume I *(Luke I–IX).* AB 28. Garden City: Doubleday, 1981.

———. "More About Elijah Coming First." *JBL* 104 (1985): 295–96.

———. *The One Who is to Come.* Grand Rapids: Eerdmans, 2007.

———. "4Q246: The 'Son of God' Document from Qumran." *Bib* 74 (1993): 153–74.

———. *A Wandering Aramean: Collected Aramaic Essays.* SBLMS 25. Missoula: Scholars, 1979.

Fraade, S. D. *From Tradition to Commentary: Torah and Its Interpretation in the Midrash Sifre to Deuteronomy.* Albany: State University of New York Press, 1991.

Frankfort, H. *Kingship and the Gods: A Study of Ancient Near Eastern Religion as the Integration of Society and Nature.* Chicago: University of Chicago Press, 1948.

Frankfurter, D. "The Legacy of Jewish Apocalypses in Early Christianity: Regional Trajectories." In *The Jewish Apocalyptic Heritage in Early Christianity*, edited by J. C. VanderKam and W. Adler. CRINT 3.4. Assen: Van Gorcum, 1996.

Fredriksen, P. *From Jesus to Christ: The Origins of the New Testament Images of Jesus*. New Haven: Yale University Press, 2000.

Freyne, S. "The Charismatic." In *Ideal Figures in Ancient Judaism: Profiles and Paradigms*, edited by J. J. Collins and G. W. E. Nickelsburg. Missoula: Scholars, 1980.

Friedman, S. "Literary Development and Historicity in the Aggadic Narrative of the Babylonian Talmud: A Study Based Upon B. M. 83b–86a." In *Community and Culture: Essays in Jewish Culture in Honor of the Ninetieth Anniversary of the Founding of Gratz College 1895–1985*, edited by N. M. Waldman. Philadelphia: Seth, 1987.

———. "Uncovering Literary Dependencies in the Talmudic Corpus." In *The Synoptic Problem in Rabbinic Literature*, edited by S. J. D. Cohen. BJS 326. Providence: Brown Judaic Studies, 2000.

Fuller, R. H. *Foundations of New Testament Christology*. Cambridge: James Clarke, 2002 [1965].

Gafni, I. M. "Concepts of Periodization and Casuality in Talmudic Literature." *Jewish History* 10 (1996): 21–38.

———. "Josephus and 1 Maccabees." In *Josephus, the Bible and History*, edited by L. H. Feldman and G. Hata. Detroit: Wayne State University Press, 1989.

Gager, J. G. *Reinventing Paul*. Oxford: Oxford University Press, 2000.

Gaston, L. *Paul and the Torah*. Vancouver: University of British Columbia Press, 1990.

Goodman, M. *Mission and Conversion: Proselytizing in the Religious History of the Roman Empire*. London: Clarendon, 1994.

Gray, R. *Prophetic Figures in Late Second Temple Jewish Palestine*. Oxford: Oxford University Press, 1993.

Green, W. S. "Palestinian Holy Men: Charismatic Leadership and Rabbinic Tradition." In *Aufstieg und Niedergang der römischen Welt: Geschichte und Kultur Roms im Spiegel der neueren Forschung*. Part 2, Principat 19.2, edited by H. Temporini and W. Haase. New York: de Gruyter, 1979.

Halperin, D. J. *The Merkabah in Rabbinic Literature*. New Haven: American Oriental Society, 1980.

Hanson, P. D. "Zechariah 9 and the Recapitulation of an Ancient Ritual Pattern." *JBL* 92 (1973): 37–59.

Hargis, J. W. *Against the Christians: The Rise of Early Anti-Christian Polemic*. New York: Peter Lang, 1999.

Harland, P. A. *Associations, Synagogues, and Congregations: Claiming a*

Place in Ancient Mediterranean Society. Minneapolis: Fortress Press, 2003.

Harnack, A. von. "Millennium." Pages 314–18 in vol. 16 of *Encyclopaedia Britannica*. 9th ed. New York: Scribner's, 1983.

Head, P. M. "A Text-Critical Study of Mark 1.1: 'The Beginning of the Gospel of Jesus Christ.'" *NTS* 37 (1991): 621–29.

Healey, J. "The Immortality of the King: Ugarit and the Psalms." *Or* 53 (1984): 245–54.

Hedner-Zetterholm, K. "Elijah's Different Roles—A Reflection of the Rabbinic Struggle for Authority." *JSQ* (forthcoming).

Hengel, M. *Between Jesus and Paul: Studies in the Earliest History of Christianity*. London: SCM Press, 1983.

———. "Christological Titles in Early Christianity." In *The Messiah: Developments in Earliest Judaism and Christianity*, edited by J. H. Charlesworth. Minneapolis: Fortress Press, 1992.

———. "Messianische Hoffnung und politischer 'Radikalismus' in der jüdisch-hellenistischen Diaspora." In *Apocalypticism in the Mediterranean World and the Near East*, edited by D. Hellholm. Tübingen: Mohr Siebeck, 1983.

Hill, C. E. "Antichrist from the Tribe of Dan." *JTS* 46 (1995): 99–117.

———. "Cerinthus, Gnostic or Chiliast? A New Solution to an Old Problem." *JECS* 8 (2000): 135–72.

———. "Marriage of Montanism and Millennialism." *StPatr* 26 (1993): 140–46.

———. "Papias of Hierapolis." *ExpTim* 117 (2006): 309–15.

———. *Regnum Caelorum: Patterns of Future Hope in Early Christianity*. Oxford: Clarendon, 1992.

Hillers, D. R. *Micah*. Hermeneia. Philadelphia: Fortress Press, 1984.

Hirshman, M. "Rabbinic Universalism in the Second and Third Centuries." *HTR* 93 (2000): 101–15.

Holmberg, B. "Jewish *Versus* Christian Identity in the Early Church." *RB* 105 (1998): 397–425.

Hooker, M. D. "'Who Can This Be?' The Christology of Mark's Gospel." In *Contours of Christology in the New Testament*, edited by R. N. Longenecker. Grand Rapids: Eerdmans, 2005.

———. *The Gospel According to Mark*. BNTC. London: A & C Black, 1993 [1991].

Horbury, W. *Jewish Messianism and the Cult of Christ*. London: SCM, 1998.

———. "The Messianic Associations of 'the Son of Man.'" In *Messianism among Jews and Christians: Twelve Biblical and Historical Studies*. London: Continuum, 2003.

————. *Messianism among Jews and Christians: Twelve Biblical and Historical Studies.* London: T&T Clark, 2003.

Horsley, R. A. "'Like One of the Prophets of Old': Two Types of Popular Prophets at the Time of Jesus." *CBQ* 47 (1985): 435–63.

————. "Popular Messianic Movements around the Time of Jesus." *CBQ* 46 (1984): 471–95.

Horsley, R. A. and J. S. Hanson, *Bandits, Prophets, and Messiahs: Popular Movements in the Time of Jesus.* Harrisburg: Trinity, 1999 [1985].

Hurtado, L. W. "Paul's Christology." In *The Cambridge Companion to St Paul*, edited by J. D. G. Dunn. Cambridge: Cambridge University Press, 2003.

Josephus. Translated by H. St. J. Thackeray et al. 10 vols. Loeb Classical Library. Cambridge: Harvard University Press, 1926–.

Joyce, P. M. "King and Messiah in Ezekiel." In *King and Messiah in Israel and the Ancient Near East.* JSOTSup 270, edited by J. Day. Sheffield: Sheffield Academic, 1998.

Juel, D. *Messianic Exegesis: Christological Interpretation of the Old Testament in Early Christianity.* Philadelphia: Fortress Press, 1992.

————. "The Origin of Mark's Christology." In *The Messiah: Developments in Earliest Judaism and Christianity*, edited by J. H. Charlesworth. Minneapolis: Fortress Press, 1992.

Keel, O. *The Symbolism of the Biblical World. Ancient Near Eastern Iconography and the Book of Psalms.* Winona Lake: Eisenbrauns, 1997.

Kim, S. *Paul and the New Perspective: Second Thoughts on the Origin of Paul's Gospel.* WUNT 140. Tübingen: Mohr Siebeck, 2002.

King, J. *Origen on the Song of Songs as the Spirit of Scripture: The Bridegroom's Perfect Marriage-Song.* Oxford Theological Monographs. New York: Oxford University Press, 2005.

Kobelski, P. J. *Melchizedek and Melchireša.* CBQMS 10. Washington: Catholic Biblical Association, 1981.

Koch, K. "Der König als Sohn Gottes in Ägypten und Israel." In *"Mein Sohn bist du" (Ps. 2,7): Studien zu den Königspsalmen*, edited by E. Otto and E. Zenger. Stuttgart: Verl. Kath. Bibelwerk, 2002.

————. "Messias und Menschensohn." In *Vor der Wende der Zeiten: Beiträge zur apokalyptischen Literatur.* Neukirchen-Vluyn: Neukirchener, 1996.

Kramer, W. *Christ, Lord, Son of God.* SBT 50. London: SCM, 1966.

Kümmel, W. G. *The Theology of the New Testament According to Its Major Witnesses Jesus — Paul — John.* London: SCM, 1987 [1972 in German].

Laato, A. *A Star is Rising: The Historical Development of the Old*

Testament Royal Ideology and the Rise of the Jewish Messianic Expectations. Atlanta: Scholars, 1997.

Ladd, G. E. *A Theology of the New Testament*. Grand Rapids: Eerdmans, 1974.

Lapin, H. "Hegemony and Its Discontents: Rabbis as a Late Antique Provincial Population." In *Jewish Culture and Society under the Christian Roman Empire*, edited by R. L. Kalmin and S. Schwartz. Leuven: Peeters, 2003.

Levenson, J. D. *Theology of the Program of Restoration of Ezekiel 40–48*. HSM 10. Missoula: Scholars, 1976.

Levey, S. H. *The Messiah: An Aramaic Interpretation: The Messianic Exegesis of the Targum*. HUCM 2. Cincinnati: Hebrew Union College/Jewish Institute of Religion, 1974.

Levine, L. I. *The Ancient Synagogue: The First Thousand Years*. New Haven: Yale University Press, 2000.

Liebers, R. *"Wie geschrieben steht": Studien zu einer besonderen Art frühchristlichen Schriftbezuges*. Berlin: de Gruyter, 1993.

Lieu, J. M. *Image and Reality: The Jews in the World of the Christians in the Second Century*. Edinburgh: T&T Clark, 1996.

———. *Neither Jew Nor Greek? Constructing Early Christianity*. London: T&T Clark, 2002.

Lindbeck, K. H. *Story and Theology: Elijah's Appearances in the Babylonian Talmud*. PhD diss., Jewish Theological Seminary, 1999.

Longenecker, R. N. "Christological Material in the Early Christian Communities." In *Contours of Christology in the New Testament*, edited by R. N. Longenecker. Grand Rapids: Eerdmans, 2005.

Luz, U. *Matthew 1–7: A Continental Commentary*. CC. Minneapolis: Fortress Press, 1989 [1985 in German].

Machinist, P. "Kingship and Divinity in Imperial Assyria." In *Text, Artifact, and Image: Revealing Ancient Israelite Religion*. BJS 346, edited by G. Beckman and T. J. Lewis. Providence: Brown Judaic Studies, 2006.

McCarter, P. K. *II Samuel: A New Translation with Introduction, Notes and Commentary*. AB 9B. Garden City: Doubleday, 1984.

McCarthy, D. "2 Samuel 7 and the Structure of the Deuteronomic History." *JBL* 84 (1985): 131–38.

McGuire, M. B. *Religion: The Social Context*. Belmont: Wadsworth, 1992.

Mekilta de R. Yismael. Edited by J. Lauterbach. 3 vols. Philadelphia: JPS, 1933–1935.

Mettinger, T. N. D. "Cui Bono? The Prophecy of Nathan (2 Sam. 7) as a Piece of Political Rhetoric." *SEÅ* 70 (2005): 193–214.

————. *King and Messiah: The Civil and Sacral Legitimation of the Israelite Kings*. ConBOT 8. Lund: Gleerup, 1976.

Milikowsky, C. "Trajectories of Return, Restoration and Redemption in Rabbinic Judaism: Elijah, the Messiah, the War of Gog and the World to Come." In *Restoration: Old Testament, Jewish, and Christian Perspectives*, edited by J. M. Scott. Leiden: Brill, 2001.

Mishnah: A New Translation With a Commentary by Rabbi Pinhas Kehati. Edited by A. Tomaschoff. 21 vols. Jerusalem: Eliner Library, 1994.

Moo, D. J. "The Christology of the Early Pauline Letters." In *Contours of Christology in the New Testament*, edited by R. N. Longenecker. Grand Rapids: Eerdmans, 2005.

Moore, G. F. "Christian Writers on Judaism." *HTR* 14 (1921): 197–254.

Moss, C. R. "The Transfiguration: An Exercise in Markan Accommodation." *BI* 12 (2004): 69–89.

Müller, U. B. *Messias und Menschensohn in jüdischen Apokalypsen und in der Offenbarung des Johannes*. Gütersloh: Mohn, 1972.

Munnich, O. "Le messianisme à la lumière des livres prophétiques de la Bible grecque." In *The Septuagint and Messianism: Colloquium Biblicum Lovaniense LIII, July 27–29, 2004*. BETL 195, edited by M. A. Knibb. Leuven: Peeters, 2006.

Nanos, M. D. *The Irony of Galatians: Paul's Letter in First Century Context*. Philadelphia: Fortress Press, 2001.

————. *The Mystery of Romans: The Jewish Context of Paul's Letter*. Minneapolis: Fortress Press, 1996.

————. "What Was at Stake in Peter's 'Eating with Gentiles' at Antioch?" In *The Galatians Debate: Contemporary Issues in Rhetorical and Historical Interpretation*, edited by M. D. Nanos. Peabody: Hendrickson, 2002.

Neusner, J. *Messiah in Context: Israel's History and Destiny in Formative Judaism*. Lanham: University Press of America, 1988.

Newman, H. I. "Jerome's Judaizers." *JECS* 9 (2000): 421–52.

Nicene and Post-Nicene Fathers, Series 2. Edited by P. Schaff and H. Wace. 1890–1900. 14 vols. Peabody: Hendrickson, 1994.

Nock, A. D. *Conversion: The Old and New in Religion from Alexander the Great to Augustine of Hippo*. Baltimore: Johns Hopkins University Press, 1998 [1933].

O'Connor, S. and D. P. Silverman, eds. *Ancient Egyptian Kingship*. Probleme der Ägyptologie 9. Leiden: Brill, 1995.

Old Testament Pseudepigrapha, Volume 1. Apocalyptic Literature and Testaments. Edited by J. H. Charlesworth. New York: Doubleday, 1983.

Old Testament Pseudepigrapha, Volume 2: Expansions of the 'Old Testament' and Legends, Wisdom and Philosophical Literature, Prayers, Psalm, and Odes, Fragments of Lost Judeo-Hellenistic Works. Edited by J. H. Charlesworth. New York: Doubleday, 1985.

Otto, E. "Politische Theologie in den Königspsalmen zwischen Ägypten und Assyrien: Die Herrscherlegitimation in den Psalmen 2 und 18 in ihrem altorientalischen Kontexten." In *"Mein Sohn bist du" (Ps. 2,7): Studien zu den Königspsalmen,* edited by E. Otto and E. Zenger. Stuttgart: Verl. Kath. Bibelwerk, 2002.

————. "Psalm 2 in neuassyrischer Zeit: Assyrische Motive in der judäischen Königsideologie." In *Textarbeit. Studien zu Texten und ihrer Rezeption aus dem Alten Testament und der Umwelt Israels.* AOAT 294, edited by K. Kiesow and T. Meurer. Münster: Ugarit, 2003.

Paul, S. M. *Amos: A Commentary on the Book of Amos.* Hermeneia, edited by F. M. Cross. Minneapolis: Fortress, 1991.

Philo. Translated by F. H. Colson and G. H. Whitaker. 10 vols. Loeb Classical Library. Cambridge: Harvard University Press, 1929–.

Plutarch. *Parallel Lives.* Translated by B. Perrin. 11 vols. Loeb Classical Library. Cambridge: Harvard University Press, 1914–.

Pomykala, K. E. *The Davidic Dynasty Tradition in Early Judaism. Its History and Significance for Messianism.* SBLEJL 7. Atlanta: Scholars, 1995.

Powell, D. "Tertullianists and Cataphrygians." *VC* 29 (1975): 33–54.

Price, S. R. F. *Religions of the Ancient Greeks: Key Themes in Ancient History.* Cambridge: Cambridge University Press, 2000.

————. "Rituals and Power." In *Paul and Empire: Religion and Power in Roman Imperial Society,* edited by R. A. Horsley. Harrisburg: Trinity, 1997.

Pucci Ben Zeev, M. *Diaspora Judaism in Turmoil, 116/117 CE: Ancient Sources and Modern Insights.* Interdisciplinary Studies in Ancient Culture and Religion 6. Leuven: Peeters, 2005.

Puech, E. "246. 4QApocryphe de Daniel ar." In *Qumran Cave 4: XVII: Parabiblical Texts, Part 3.* DJD XXII, edited by G. Brooke et al. Oxford: Clarendon, 1996.

————. "Fragments d'un apocryphe de Lévi et le personage eschatologique: 4QTest Lévi c-d (?) et 4QAJa." In *The Madrid Qumran Congress (STDJ* 11), edited by J. Trebolle Barrera and L. Vegas Montaner. Leiden: Brill, 1992.

Rad, G. von. *Old Testament Theology.* 2 vols. New York: Harper & Row, 1965.

———. "The Royal Ritual in Judah." In *The Problem of the Hexateuch and other Essays*, edited by G. von Rad. New York: McGraw-Hill, 1966.

Rajak, T. "Jewish Millenarian Expectations." In *The First Jewish Revolt: Archaeology, History and Ideology*, edited by A. M. Berlin and J. A. Overman. London: Routledge, 2002.

Rambo, L. R. *Understanding Religious Conversion*. New Haven: Yale University Press, 1993.

Roberts, J. J. M. "The Old Testament's Contribution to Messianic Expectations." In *The Messiah: Developments in Earliest Judaism and Christianity*, edited by J. H. Charlesworth. Philadelphia: Fortress Press, 1992.

———. "Whose Child is This? Reflections on the Speaking Voice in Isaiah 9:5." *HTR* 90 (1997): 115–29.

Rubenstein, J. L. "Criteria of Stammaitic Intervention in Aggada." In *Creation and Composition: The Contribution of the Bavli Redactors (Stammaim) to the Aggada*, edited by J. L. Rubenstein, Tübingen: Mohr, 2005.

———. *The Culture of the Babylonian Talmud*. Baltimore: Johns Hopkins University Press, 2003.

———. *Talmudic Stories: Narrative Art, Composition, and Culture*. Baltimore: Johns Hopkins University Press, 1999.

Runesson, A. *The Origins of the Synagogue: A Socio-Historical Study*. ConBNT 37. Stockholm: Almqvist & Wiksell, 2001.

Sanders, E. P. "Jewish Associations with Gentiles and Galatians 2:11–14." In *The Conversation Continues: Studies in Paul and John in Honour of J. Louis Martyn*, edited by R. T. Fortna and B. R. Gaventa. Nashville: Abingdon, 1990.

———. *Paul and Palestinian Judaism: A Comparison of Patterns of Religion*. Minneapolis: Fortress Press, 1977.

Schäfer, P. "Aqiva and Bar Kokhba." In *Approaches to Ancient Judaism: Volume II*. BJS 9, edited by W. S. Green. Atlanta: Scholars, 1980.

———. *Der Bar Kokhba Aufstand: Studien zum zweiten jüdischen Krieg gegen Rom*. TSAJ 1. Tübingen: Mohr Siebeck, 1981.

Schaper, J. *Eschatology in the Greek Psalter*. WUNT 76. Tübingen: Mohr Siebeck, 1995.

Schauss, H. *The Jewish Festivals: History and Observance*. New York: Schocken, 1938.

Schniedewind, W. M. *Society and the Promise to David: The Reception History of 2 Samuel 7:1–17*. New York: Oxford University Press, 1999.

Schwartz, S. *Imperialism and Jewish Society, 200 BCE to 640 CE* Princeton: Princeton University Press, 2001.

Shiner, W. T. "The Ambiguous Pronouncement of the Centurion and the Shrouding of Meaning in Mark." *JSNT* 78 (2000): 3–22.

Shiner, W. T., and D. E. Aune. "Christian Prophecy and the Messianic Status of Jesus." In *The Messiah: Developments in Earliest Judaism and Christianity*, edited by J. H. Charlesworth. Minneapolis: Fortress Press, 1992.

Slee, M. *The Church in Antioch in the First Century CE: Communion and Conflict.* JSNTSup 244. London: Sheffield Academic, 2003.

Smith, C. R. "Chiliasm and Recapitulation in the Theology of Ireneus." *VC* 48 (1994): 313–31.

Smyth, H. W. *Greek Grammar.* Rev. by G. M. Messing. Cambridge: Harvard University Press, 1956.

Starcky, J. "Les quatres étapes du messianisme à Qumrân." *RB* 70 (1963): 481–505.

Stark, R. *Cities of God: The Real Story of How Christianity Became an Urban Movement and Conquered Rome.* New York: HarperSanFrancisco, 2006.

———. *The Rise of Christianity: How the Obscure, Marginal Jesus Movement Became the Dominant Religious Force in the Western World in a Few Centuries.* San Francisco: HarperCollins, 1997.

Stendahl, K. *Final Account: Paul's Letter to the Romans.* Minneapolis: Fortress Press, 1995.

———. *Paul among Jews and Gentiles, and Other Essays.* Philadelphia: Fortress Press, 1976.

Stone, M. E. *Fourth Ezra: A Commentary on the Book of Fourth Ezra.* Hermeneia, edited by F. M. Cross. Minneapolis: Fortress Press, 1990.

Stowers, S. K. *A Rereading of Romans: Justice, Jews and Gentiles.* New Haven: Yale University Press, 1994.

Strack, H. L., and P. Billerbeck. *Kommentar zum Neuen Testament aus Talmud und Midrasch.* München: Beck, 1926.

Sweeney, M. A. *Isaiah 1–39 with an Introduction to Prophetic Literature.* FOTL 16. Grand Rapids: Eerdmans, 1996.

———. *King Josiah of Judah: The Lost Messiah of Israel.* Oxford: Oxford University Press, 2001.

Talmon, S. "The Concept of *Māšîaḥ* and Messianism in Early Judaism." In *The Messiah: Developments in Earliest Judaism and Christianity*, edited by J. H. Charlesworth. Minneapolis: Fortress Press, 1992.

Tellbe, M. *Paul between Synagogue and State: Christians, Jews, and Civic Authorities in 1 Thessalonians, Romans, and Philippians.* ConBNT 34. Stockholm: Almqvist & Wiksell, 2001.

Trevett, C. *Montanism: Gender, Authority and the New Prophecy.* Cambridge: Cambridge University Press, 1996.

Turcan, R. *The Gods of Ancient Rome: Religion in Everyday Life from Archaic to Imperial Times.* New York: Routledge, 2001 [1998 in French].

Urbach, E. E. *The Sages: Their Concepts and Beliefs.* Jerusalem: Magnes, 1987.

Vermes, G. *The Changing Faces of Jesus.* Penguin Compass. New York: Penguin, 2002.

———. *The Complete Dead Sea Scrolls in English.* Rev. ed. London: Penguin, 2004.

———. "Hanina Ben Dosa: A Controversial Galilean Saint from the First Century of the Christian Era (II)." *JJS* 24 (1973): 51–64.

———. *Jesus the Jew: A Historian's Reading of the Gospels.* London: Collins, 1973.

Viberg, Å. *Symbols of Law: A Contextual Analysis of Legal Symbolic Acts in the Old Testament.* ConBOT 32. Stockholm: Almqvist & Wiksell, 1976.

Wegner, P. D. *An Examination of Kingship and Messianic Expectation in Isaiah 1–35.* Lewiston: Mellen, 1992.

Wellhausen, J. *Die Kleinen Propheten übersetzt und erklärt.* Berlin: Reiner, 1898.

Wildberger, H. *Isaiah 1–12: A Commentary.* Minneapolis: Fortress Press, 1991.

Wilken, R. *The Christians as the Romans Saw Them.* New Haven: Yale University Press, 1984.

———. "Early Christian Chiliasm, Jewish Messianism, and the Idea of the Holy Land." *HTR* 79 (1986): 298–307.

Williamson, H. G. M. "The Messianic Texts in Isaiah 1–39." In *King and Messiah in Israel and the Ancient Near East.* JSOTSup 270, edited by J. Day. Sheffield: Sheffield Academic, 1998.

———. *Variations on a Theme: King, Messiah and Servant in the Book of Isaiah.* Carlisle: Paternoster, 1998.

Wise, M. O. *The First Messiah: Investigating the Savior before Christ.* San Francisco: HarperSanFrancisco, 1999.

Wolff, H. W. *Joel and Amos: A Commentary on the Books of the Prophets Joel and Amos.* Hermeneia, edited by S. D. McBride. Philadelphia: Fortress Press, 1977.

Wright, N. T. "Paul's Gospel and Caesar's Empire." In *Paul and Politics: Ekklesia, Israel, Imperium, Interpretation: Essays in honor of Krister Stendahl*, edited by R. A. Horsley. Harrisburg: Trinity, 2000.

Wyatt, N. *Myths of Power: A Study of Royal Myth and Ideology in Ugaritic and Biblical Tradition*. Münster: Ugarit, 1996.

Xeravits, G. G. *King, Priest, Prophet: Positive Eschatological Protagonists of the Qumran Library*. STDJ 47. Leiden: Brill, 2003.

Yerushalmi, Y. H. *Zakhor: Jewish History and Jewish Memory*. Seattle and London: University of Washington Press, 1982.

Zetterholm, M. *The Formation of Christianity in Antioch: A Social-Scientific Approach to the Separation between Judaism and Christianity*. Routledge Early Church Monographs. London: Routledge, 2003.

—————. "Purity and Anger: Gentiles and Idolatry in Antioch." *Interdisciplinary Journal of Research on Religion* 1:Article 10 (2005): 1–24.

Zimmermann, J. *Messianische Texte aus Qumran: Königliche, priesterliche und prophetische Messiasvorstellungen in den Schriftfunden von Qumran*. WUNT 2/104. Tübingen: Mohr Siebeck, 1998.

Index of Passages

157

Index of Modern Authors